Dreaming of the "Signs"

A Treasury of
Georgia Folklore

By
Ronald G. Killion
and
Charles T. Waller

Illustrations by
Maureen O'Leary

CHEROKEE PUBLISHING COMPANY

ATLANTA

"The Library of Congress catalogued the first
issue of this title as follows:"
Killion, Ronald G., comp.
A treasury of Georgia folk-lore, by Ronald G. Killion and
Charles T. Waller. Illus. by Maureen O'Leary.   Atlanta, Chero-
kee Pub. Co., 1972.

267 p.   illus.   24 cm. $10.00

Prose and poems.
"Composed of materials collected by the Georgia Writer's Project from 1936
to 1940."

1. Folklore—Georgia.   2. Georgia—Social life and customs.   I. Waller,
Charles T., joint comp.   II. Title.

GR110.G4K54   398.2'09758   72-88901
                                                                MARC

Library of Congress   72[8208r82]rev

This book is printed on acid-free paper which conforms to the American
National Standard Z39.48-1984 *Permanence of Paper for Printed Library
Materials.* Paper that conforms to this standard's requirements for pH, alka-
line reserve and freedom from groundwood is anticipated to last several
hundred years without significant deterioration under normal library use
and storage conditions.

Manufactured in the United States of America
ISBN: 978-0-87797-022-4 Hardcover
ISBN: 978-0-87797-298-3 Paper
Copyright 1972 by
Ronald G. Killion
and
Charles T. Waller

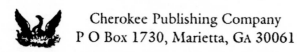

Cherokee Publishing Company
P O Box 1730, Marietta, GA 30061

For
Pearl and Tom

TABLE OF CONTENTS

A TREASURY OF
GEORGIA FOLKLORE

PREFACE

The Federal Writer's Project, a division of the Works Progress Administration, was created in 1935 under the Emergency Relief Appropriations Act as a part of President Franklin Roosevelt's New Deal. Some executive in Washington saw an opportunity to use brain power in addition to the muscle power on the federal payroll. Writers in each state were made into field workers and assigned numerous tasks, the first of which was the writing of a guidebook to each state, a successful venture printed as the American Guide Series, of which *Georgia: A Guide to its Towns and Countryside*, published by the University of Georgia Press in 1940, is one.

The second major task of the WPA Writer's Project was the collection of folklore. A few state groups hurried some collections into print, but 1941 saw the end of most of the folklore projects, and thousands of pages of valuable manuscript material were stuffed into boxes and placed in various archives and libraries across the nation. The fate of those papers is generally a sad one, as most of them were either destroyed or lost.

From several living field workers, we have pieced together the following information about Georgia's collection: there were certainly two, and maybe three large boxes of material, disorderly and uncatalogued, but nevertheless valuable. A former area supervisor says that one box found its way to Atlanta; the Georgia Archives or the Atlanta Public Library may have received it. We have searched extensively, but we have not yet been able to locate those papers.

The second box went to the University of Georgia library. The Special Collections Department of the library, now under the watchful eyes of John Bonner and Mrs. William Tate, has kept the material available for the use of the folklorist through all these years. It is a part of this collection which we have tried to organize into book form.

The task of editing this material, however, was formidable. Unorganized, untitled, often unsigned, the manuscripts may best be described as folklore notes. One typical page consists of a possible plantation song, a nonsense rhyme, several folk cures, a children's game and some random comments, all by an unnamed informant. Across the top of the page, written in pencil, in a left-leaning script is the notation, "Notes made by Mrs. Dillard (State Director) on trips over state." Here is a page from the manuscript:

FOLK-LORE AND FOLK-SONG

Overwhelmed by the frenzy of a "holy dance," a Negro Minister panted: "You sees me dancin', folks, but de skip's on de inside." This Negro Minister was an experienced "hoodo-doctor," and believed in "de signs an' wonders."

Being present once at the burning down of a Negro home, a small girl was sorrowfully watching the flames consume the family possessions, all the while wailing the most doleful sound:

> *Oh Lawd, Papa had some matches,*
> *Took an' lef' 'em in de closet, Lawd,*
> *Cotch'd all de clothes on fiah, Lawd,*
> *No throwed on watah, Lawd*
> *Couldn't put hit out, Lawd,*
> *Couldn't put his out!*
> *An' all Papa's things done burned!*

Silver seems to play an important part in Negro folklore, which holds that ghosts may be killed with silver bullets and the spirit may be kept in the grave by screwing the coffin lid down with silver screws.

A tale is told of a woman who had unknowingly married the devil and gone with him to hell; she sees her mother rise from the grave and turn to a silver knife and her father to a silver dish.

––––––

With such material the editors were confronted with two primary problems: how to make the book enjoyable for the general reader and yet still present it so that the folklorist might find it useful in his work without spending hundreds of hours combing through manuscripts. We decided that a topical division of the material was the only solution to the first problem.

Our greatest scholarly problems were these:

(1) Dialect. Many of the folklore papers, like the numerous interviews with former slaves, were written in heavy Southern dialect, each field worker using his own transcription. When we tested these dialect papers on our own college students, we found that, for the most part, the modern young person finds written Southern dialect both frightening and unintelligible. Indeed, even the editors hesitated over such sentences as "Gosties kin be kilt only wid uh sibber bullit." We have therefore changed spelling often, but seldom word order, diction, or grammar. We hope we have kept the suggestion of the dialect while making the material available for the modern reader.

(2) Selection. With over 3,000 pages of manuscript, one great concern has been that of selection. Much could immediately be set aside, *i.e.*, the essays on fish fries or church socials, or histories of flag day which, while often interesting and well-written, were of only peripheral concern. We dismissed much historical material as relevant for another book, but not this one. Where history became legend, as in the cases of Nancy Hart and Robert Toombs, the editors have used personal judgment. Over a hundred tales of supernatural visitation have been reduced to a catalog of Georgia ghosts, but we have retained a few tales as representative.

In those chapters consisting primarily of lists (Folk Medicine, Superstitions, Folk Wisdom, *etc.*) we have been inclusive. The lists represent all we could reasonably find on one item, although we are equally sure that something is missing. In some hidden corner of some interview there is bound to be another cure for whooping cough or diptheria that we have overlooked.

Finally, the economic factor has dictated that much of interest be omitted. The editors have often been forced to choose between two equally good stories, or songs, or anecdotes, and the choice often rested simply on personal preference.

(3) Notes. The editors have included wherever possible all information concerning the informant, his area of the state, the date of the interview or the manuscript, and the field worker's name. Complete information almost never exists. Almost half the papers regrettably contain no information whatsoever about the informants. We have therefore left without notation the material presented without identification of informants rather than con-

cern the reader with numerous references to "anonymous informant" or "field worker's name not included."

The only exception to this principle of notation occurs in the chapters consisting primarily of listed items. The footnote is often longer than the items involved; notation for each would lengthen the book by about one-third. We have therefore compromised by listing only the most important sources for these chapters.

The book is designed for the popular reader, however, and primarily for the Georgian whose rich hertiage it is. For those old enough, this anthology is something to remember; for those too young, it is an antique. For the editors, the material has provided a great number of hours of fun.

Until now, no single printed volume has centered on Georgia's folklore. *A Treasury of Georgia Folklore* is composed of materials collected by the Georgia Writer's Project from 1936 to 1940. The informants were anyone over the state who could or would contribute—housewives, small-town merchants, professional men, farmers, plantation owners, servants, or former Negro slaves. Roughly two-thirds of the informants were Negroes. The resulting collection reflects a way of life which existed in the state for about eighty years, from the 1860's (the earliest even the oldest informant could remember) to the beginning of World War II. The material included here should be of interest to historians and sociologists as well as folklorists because it was gathered at the end of the Depression and before the advent of television or the changes wrought by the war. Never again can one collect this sort of source material. The world it reflects has been shrinking very fast.

To Professor Janet M. DuBois the authors offer their gratitude for help with the chapter on folk music and the preparation of the manuscript. We are grateful to Mary Ann Bratt for many hours of manuscript typing. Finally, we offer our sincere thanks to the numerous field workers who gathered the folk data: Maude Barragan, Martha G. Bell, John N. Booth, Lucille Bridges, Henrietta Carlisle, Mary A. Crawford, Ruth A. Chitty, William Kermit Dekle, M. H. Dauphin, L. S. Doughty, Elizabeth Driskell, Harriet Hallworth, Mary Ann Hall, J. R. Jones, Marion V. Kumar, Mary Lawton, W. W. Linton, Edith Bell Love, W. C. Massey,

Louise Oliphant, George Paulk, Dorothy Plagwitze, Ruby Lorraine Radford, M. B. Ross, Olin Sneed, Nan Bagby Stephens, J. Swilling, R. Stonestreet, Hattie Taylor and George M. Ward.

Athens, Georgia
15 May 1972

Ronald Gene Killion
Charles Thomas Waller

GEORGIA:
ITS PEOPLE AND ITS FOLKLORE

The native Georgian finds reminders of his state's past around him everywhere. He remembers the Indians from place names like Annawakee, Nacoochee, Warwoman Road, Four Killer's Creek and Standing Boy Branch. The early settlers here as elsewhere identified various sites with uninspired repetitions of Dry Creek, Golden Cove, Pine Level, or Devil's Cave, but they left some fascinating originals too: Eastertoy Settlement, Snapfinger Road, Po' Biddy Crossroad, Useless Bay, Lordamercy Cave, Child Toaters Creek, Milksick Cove, No Man's Friend Pond, and at least three places called Hard Labor. Georgia's place names recall the cosmopolitan nature of its settlers—Natal, Mt. Asia, Rome, Ypsilanti, Egypt, Geneva, and Athens. Even Georgia's military past remains with us in Breastwork Branch where Andrew Jackson's men encamped, and in Little Intrenchment Creek, which has now been inundated by Lake Lanier and will probably soon pass from memory.

What will never pass, however, is the richness of Georgia's folklore and its continuing life, even in an increasingly urban society. The folklorist often receives a surprised reaction when some informant discovers he is singing a song or telling a story or repeating an adage which is a part of the living traditions of folk literature. "Son," an elderly mountaineer from Blairsville once said when informed that he had just recited a piece of folklore, "you call it whatever you like, but to me it's jest plain living. I been hearing that story since I could remember."

That, of course, is the whole point. Folklore is the study of the oral tradition of any culture, and a region's folklore is often as distinctive as anything else about the culture. By its very nature folklore is living history, keeping the past alive by the tale, song, proverb, or barnyard metaphor as they are known and repeated by the common man. To grasp the elusive experience of this past is the task of the folklorist, and when that past has been as rich as Georgia's the task seems all the more difficult.

When the first Europeans entered Georgia they found the land inhabited by two main nations of Indians, the Cherokees in the North and the Creeks over the remainder of the state. The latter tribe included the Yamasee, Tomali, Natchez, and Uchee. The

1

Indians have long since left Georgia, but their traditions remain as part of the nature lore and folk superstitions learned by the earliest European settlers. Georgia's topography remembers them, too, for hardly a stream or a mountain does not have some connected legend like the Chattahoochee (Flowered Rock), Hiawassee (Pretty Fawn), Tallulah (Terrible One) Falls; we still fish and swim and drink the water from streams and rivers they first named—the Oconee, the Ogeechee, the Ocmulgee.

When DeSoto entered Georgia in 1540, looking for a mythical Golden City, he opened the wilderness to a period called the Golden Age of Spanish Missions in eastern Georgia. These out-posts, consisting of only a few priests and some soldiers, were designed to serve as a defense against the French and English in the North, and for a while they succeeded, even under frequent attack from English pirates. Beginning with the islands of St. Catherines, Cumberland, and St. Simons, the area of Guale (Spain's name for Georgia) eventually included missions as far as Columbus, Spain's northernmost hold in the New World.

Meanwhile, the English settlements crept down the Atlantic seaboard with a regularity which disturbed the Spanish. The French tried to enter Georgia from their settlement in Louisiana, and old French maps even give the area the name of Louisiana, but their holdings were never extensive, consisting primarily of trading posts and an occasional small fort. Thus, in pre-colonial days Georgia was disputed land, and all three great European powers—Spain, France, and England—laid claim to her.

Spain watched anxiously the English colony at Jamestown in 1607 and recognized the right of England to settle in South Carolina in 1670, but it was willing to fight if there were any further entrenchment on its land. Oglethorpe in 1733 brought 135 settlers to Savannah and eventually defeated the Spanish in the Battle of Bloody Marsh in 1742. The Spanish then withdrew to Florida, and today the only visible reminders of Spanish Georgia are the tabby ruins along the coast. A few place names, some legends, several superstitions, and the myth of a fabulous Spanish stone called Boyano's Diamond have become a part of Georgia folklore.

The European settlers who arrived in America brought with them a host of superstitions and beliefs. Both the educated and the uneducated believed in a world filled with witches, devils, and demons, and they regulated their lives accordingly. In eighteenth-century England Queen Anne herself held days of visitation when she would lay her hands on sick children to heal by the traditional supernatural power of the crown. Every English village was over-run by demons and ghosts, and Jack-o-de-Lantern regularly wandered about the countryside. Buckeyes were carried in the left pocket to ward off evil or to cure rheumatism, and hens were never allowed to set an odd number of eggs. The Englishmen who came to Georgia did not forget either their law or their lore.

Soon, however, Georgia became a great melting pot for European settlers. Forty Hebrews arrived in late 1733 and later a band of German Salzburgers paved the way for a vast German immigration which even outnumbered the English in the next decade. The hard-working German Lutherans brought their Christian ethics with them, and many of the moral aphorisms contained in this collection can be traced to German origin. The loudmouth is still advised by the German proverb, "If you cackle, lay," and the judgment of the lazy remains the German adage, "It's a poor sheep that can't carry its own wool."

Scotch Highlanders arrived in Darien in 1735, and they were followed by the Irish, the Italians, the Swiss, and the Portuguese. Even in the earliest years Georgia soil saw worship by the Jews, Anglicans, Presbyterians, Roman Catholics, Lutherans, Baptists, and Moravians. Within two decades of its founding as a colony, the population of Georgia was as cosmopolitan as could be found anywhere in the New World.

Bt 1745 Georgia's plantation period had begun with the growing of mulberry trees for the silk worm. The settlers were particularly pleased when Queen Caroline wore a gown made of Georgia silks. Soon, however, the introduction of African slaves changed Georgia's economy. Cheap labor turned the plantation owners to rice as a major money crop, and rice plantations arose on the islands and along the coastal rivers. A second great change occurred in 1793 when Eli Whitney invented the cotton gin at Mulberry Grove plantation near Savannah. By 1826 Georgia had become the world's chief source of cotton. It possessed in the nineteenth century more plantations than any other Southern state, and the romantic picture of the Southern belle and beau, the easy life of the planter, and their rich traditions can be traced in fact as well as fiction.

The introduction of African slaves provided Georgia with yet another major influence in its folklore, and that influence has been considerable. Fanny Kemble in her famous *Journal of a Residence on a Georgia Plantation in 1838-1839* mentions work songs and spirituals and the excellent animal fictions of the Southern Negro. However, the folklorist has been too quick to identify this Negro folklore as entirely of African origin. European customs and folk beliefs had the great advantage of language; the white man saw no need to learn a tribal dialect, but the slave had no such choice. Most of what is casually identified as African can be traced to a European origin. Negro folklore in Georgia is an adaptation of European, native American, and African folk materials as developed under slavery and then quasi-freedom; a grafting of old world beliefs and customs onto the Georgia cultural patterns and environment.

A balancing force of culture at the time was derived from Georgia's frontier. Cheap land and a warm climate brought in settlers at the turn of the nineteenth century from every country in Europe, and also from Virginia and the Carolinas. Georgia's population rose from 83,000 in 1790 to 350,000 in 1820, and by the middle of the century there were a million Georgians. The aristocrats and slaves were still located primarily along the eastern coast. The majority of the newcomers were farmers who struggled with their land to make a living for themselves and their families. As late as 1860 only 2,858 Georgians were listed as planters (owners of twenty slaves or more) rather than farmers.

These years of rapid development saw the pushing back of the Southern frontier and the development of a crude rural culture which has come to be identified more with the West than the South. Georgia's frontier was as rough if not as large as that across the Mississippi. In 1835 Georgia jurist-teacher-ecclesiastic Augustus B. Longstreet published *Georgia Scenes*, America's first fully-developed description of frontier life with its crude humor and exotic values. The corn-shuckings, the good-natured ear-bitings and eye-gougings, the free-for-all fights during court week, the church gatherings and revivals, the fox hunts, and the shooting matches—all of these reflected the frontier civilization of which he was a part in Georgia.

Georgia's varied folklore is derived from its land as well as its people. The largest state east of the Mississippi, Georgia is divided into five distinct topographical zones which have provided more than scenic variety. The land has made the mountain man different from the swamp dweller, and the coastal farmer has little in common with the South Georgia rancher. The water routes of the southwestern part of the state join those leading to Florida's gulf coast for economic reasons, and the rich and unique culture of Georgia's mountaineers can partially be traced to the area's inaccessibility. The names of the topographical zones—the Cumberland Plateau, the Appalachian Valley, the Appalachian Mountains, the Piedmont Plateau, and the Coastal Plateau—indicate that Georgia consists of lovely mountains, rich valleys, rolling plateaus, dense swamps, clay hills, semi-tropical islands, flat savannahs, and thick pine forests.

The Civil War (1861-1865) changed the direction of Georgia's social and political development, and its cultural patterns followed. The turmoil of battle was followed by the Reconstruction years and the final demise of the plantation culture. Folklore developed around both carpetbaggers and lumber gangs, the freed Negro and the Ku Klux Klan, the proud ruined planter and the rising middle-class merchant. Georgia was on its way toward the twentieth century.

For many people its arrival came too fast. Skyscrapers quickly replaced Greek revival mansions, and one finds it increasingly difficult to locate a magnolia or a peach tree within our cities. The hoop-skirted Georgia belle now wears a mini-skirt to her office in one of the industrial complexes which dot Atlanta. We have become somewhat estranged from the folklore of our past; we have even become self-conscious about it. However, in both the bustle of city living and the slower pace of the country, Georgia's rich folklore traditions continue. This book is the editors' reminder of those traditions.

CHAPTER I

GEORGIA FOLK TALES

Georgians have always been good story tellers. The early Indians fabricated for De Soto and his men a tale of an empire of gold set in a mountain valley; early European travelers described animals and people who lived in the area as creatures with four heads and fabulous shapes; the early Crackers developed a rough frontier humor which startled delicate visitors; and the slaves brought from Africa a mythology which evolved on the plantation into the tales of Uncle Remus.

Although the modern technological society has severely limited the folktale tradition, it has not succeded in destroying it. The bawdy joke, of course, remains with us forever. The hunter who swears he bagged three quail with one shot, and the fisherman who lost a fish "this long" simply carry on a lively American folk tradition called the brag tale. The lost ring story (coin, earring, goldpiece, *etc.*) still wanders around the lakes and streams of Georgia where, after losing the item, a fisherman catches a bass a year later at the same spot. As expected, when the fish is cleaned, there inside is the lost ring. Even the comments on Georgia's changeable weather simply provide continuity for the tall tale. In some North Georgia counties natives insist that summer flowers bloom on the Southern slopes of the mountains while the Northern slopes are still covered by snow.

With the richness and variety of the state's past the folklorist would be surprised to find anything less than great folktales. The Indians, the cosmopolitan colonists, the planters, the slaves, the Crackers—all Georgians have contributed to and enjoyed the folktale tradition. Augustus Longstreet's *Georgia Scenes* (1835) was the first major book in America to develop and popularize frontier humor, and Joel Chandler Harris' *Uncle Remus* (1880) made famous the myths of both men and animals. At least two

7

Georgians have moved from history to the more nebulous land of folklore: the legends of Nancy Hart, Georgia's Revolutionary heroine, and Robert Toombs, the great unreconstructed rebel, still abound wherever storytelling occasions arise.

Storytelling in Georgia was a popular social activity during the years which gave up this collection of tales. Good storytellers quickly gained reputations, and often stories would be attributed to some raconteur who had never even heard the tale. Uncle Ben was a plantation favorite in South Georgia around Thomasville, and a fellow called Obe White was supposed to spin the best yarns in the mountains of the northeast. Then, as now, the country elections and court sessions, weddings, funerals, fairs, and church functions were all occasions for social gathering. Here men and women transacted business, exchanged news, and told anecdotes, jokes and stories. This collection consists of some of those tales which have been the good neighbors and pleasant companions of Georgians for generations.

Indian Tales[1]

DeSoto and the Pearls[2]

In the spring of 1539 Hernando de Soto, following his famous trip to Florida in search of the Fountain of Youth, came to Georgia worn and exhausted after a hazardous trip through the swamps of southern Georgia. The expedition finally reached the province of Cutifachiqui, an Indian province ruled by a rich and beautiful queen. The Spaniards were hospitably received by the queen, who entertained them at her village and showered them with gifts.

Not satisfied with this, the rapacious Spaniards stripped the temples and burying places of their treasures, to the great chagrin of the queen, who was helpless to do anything to prevent it. Finally, hearing that the queen's mother, a widow who lived many leagues away, was the possessor of some valuable pearls, DeSoto sent a party to obtain them by force. The guide for this party was an Indian youth, a protege of the old queen and the only person who knew the place where she was hiding from the Spaniards.

DeSoto Seeks The Indians' Pearls

The young Indian was a proud and gallant youth. His head was decorated with lofty plumes of different colored feathers; he wore a mantle of dressed deer-skin; in his hand he bore a beautiful bow so highly varnished that it appeared to be enameled, and each separate arrow in his quiver was a work of art as well as a skillful weapon. When halfway to the old queen's hiding place, the Indian youth suddenly stabbed himself with the finest arrow, which had a point of flint, long and sharp and shaped like a dagger, to prevent himself from betraying his benefactor.

Unable to find the old queen, the Spaniards concentrated upon securing the remaining treasure of the Cutifachiqui. The outraged young queen refused further assistance when DeSoto resumed his march once more; consequently, she and her maidens were taken prisoner and forced to accompany the expedition in order to obtain more assistance from her subjects. At length, in North Georgia, the young queen is said to have escaped, but legend doesn't say whether she ever returned to her tribe.

The Miracle of the Lakes[3]

Whenever the Creek Indians, once the inhabitants of South Georgia, displeased the Great Spirit who watched over their hunting and fishing, he caused the waters of all the lakes, meaning Lakes Jackson, Immonia, Miccousukee, and Hall, lying immediately to the South of Thomasville, to suddenly disappear. At intervals, whenever the Indians failed to make proper and timely sacrifices to this Spirit, either one or more of these lakes would dry up. Once when Lake Miccousukee had dried up, a strange Medicine Man came to the Indian camp, on what had been the shore of the lake and, seeing the Indians depressed and their own medicine men performing some ceremony intended to cause the lake to refill, asked what was the cause of their distress. Upon being told, he immediately stated that he could cause the lake to rise again. Naturally the Indians of the Camp were overjoyed but skeptical. But as their own Medicine Men had failed, he was invited to try. Near a high bluff a short distance from the camp was a small pool, all that was left of the vast lake. This Medicine Man asked that each warrior bring to him at the bluff ten large rocks the size of a man. The finding of these was not difficult since the area is covered with lime-stone. Transportation of the rocks to the high bluff was a problem; however, in due course the task was completed. Each warrior was requested to cast his rocks from the bluff into the pool under the direction of this man. The waters gradually began to rise, and in a few days the lake had returned to normal. The Indians were overjoyed; they made many gifts to the stranger in the belief that he possessed a medicine powerful enough to cause the lake to fill again with water. The Medicine Man went away, the Indians believing he had returned to the Great Spirit who had sent him. Who he was or what sent him is a mystery. The Medicine Man, evidently having studied the situation, perhaps even possessing some natural engineering ability, knew the cause of the situation. There was an opening in the small pool, sufficient in size to very nearly permit the outflow of the same amount of water as was flowing into the lake. Obstructions had already begun to form in the hole, and the Indian simply hastened this by filling the opening with large rocks. Today if one carefully examines a rock formation near this bluff, he will be surprised to learn that the rocks lying on the bottom and so plainly seen through shallow water, are not there by an act of nature, but were put there carefully and most effectively by some human agency.

Legend of Thundering Springs[4]

In Upson County there remains a legend explaining the origin of Thundering Springs.

A young Indian chieftain, Bian-wa-wa, lived with members of his tribe in the foothills of Pine Mountain near a crystal-clear spring. On a hunting expedition one day he was wounded and carried to the village of a Cherokee chieftain whose beautiful daughter Theotaska cared for him. They fell in love but the girl's father would not permit her to marry into another tribe.

Bian-wa-wa returned to his tribe alone but later came back to the Cherokee village and stole Theotaska away to his home, where a wedding feast was held amid great rejoicing. They lived together by the spring for several years before a warrior from a distant tribe came bearing news of an Indian war, and Bian-wa-wa with his braves again went on the war path. During the months following most of the young warriors returned, but not Bian-wa-wa.

Theotaska, grieving over the absence of her husband, slowly wasted away and died. She was buried on a knoll near the spring.

One winter night several years later the few remaining Indians were startled to see a man ride into the village on horseback. The rider was Bian-wa-wa. He had been captured during battle and was just released.

When he learned of his wife's death, his grief was so great that he spurred his horse and plunged down the hillside into the glittering spring below. The Great Spirit, pitying his anguish, let the horse and its rider sink into the bottomless spring and he was never seen again. For many generations the moaning of Bian-wa-wa could be heard beneath the water, like the sound of distant thunder. During the last half of the nineteenth century this moaning stopped and it is believed that Bian-wa-wa has found Theotaska.

Legend of Cohutta Mountain[5]

Cohutta Mountain in Murray County is the locale of the Cherokee myth known as the legend of Agan-Unitsi and the Uktena.

Agan-Unitsi (Ground Hog's Mother), a great medicine man of the Shawano tribe, was captured by the Cherokees and condemned to death by torture. He begged for his life, saying that if he were spared he would find for them the great wonder worker, the Ulunsutui, a blazing gem set in the forehead of Uktena, the great serpent.

The Uktena waited for its victims in the dark passes of the Great Smoky Mountains. Agan-Unitsi knew of this and began his search. While journeying southward he came upon many large reptiles, but they were not what he was seeking. At last on Gahuti (Cohutta) Mountain he found the Uktena asleep.

He hastened down the mountainside as fast as he could and when near the bottom he stopped to build a large circle of pine cones, inside which he dug a deep trench. After setting fire to the pine cones he hastened back up the mountain. Finding the great serpent still asleep he drew his bow and pierced its heart with an arrow. The snake reared its head and rushed at him, but the great hunter ran down the mountain side, jumped the circle of fire, and lay down in the trench.

The Uktena tried to follow him but fell dead before the ring of fire, and its body rolled down the steep slope, breaking trees in its path, until it reached the bottom. Agan-Unitsi called the birds and beasts to a feast which lasted until there was not a morsel left.

After seven days the magician returned to the spot one night and found the great diamond gleaming in the darkness. Wrapping it carefully, he took it with him back to the camp of the Cherokees and from that time he was regarded as one of the great medicine men of his tribe.

Legend of Ustutli

There was once a great serpent that made its haunt upon Cohutta Mountain. It was called Ustutli, or foot snake, because it had feet at both ends of its body and moved over the ground like a gigantic measuring-worm. This mighty serpent was said to be so large that it could cross large ravines by throwing its head across, getting a firm grip with its front feet and then swinging its body over. It could bleat like a fawn, and whenver an Indian hunter would hear a fawn bleat he would become frightened and hasten back to his camp.

In time not a hunter in the vicinity of Cohutta would venture upon the mountain for dread of this great serpent. At last a man from one of the northern tribes came there to visit some relatives. When the ceremonial feast of welcome was prepared for him there were only corn and beans to eat, and the host explained that there was no meat because the hunters were afraid to go into the mountains. The visitor declared that he would go himself on the morrow and either bring in a deer or kill the Ustutli. They tried to dissuade him, but as he insisted on going they warned him that if he came upon it he must run around the side of the mountain instead of straight down because the weight of the great serpent's body made it difficult for it to travel around the base of the steep slopes.

In the morning the hunter left and had not travelled far when he heard the bleat of a fawn. Pushing on through the brush he soon saw the monster directly in front of him.

The hunter was so terribly frightened that he turned and fled down the mountainside, the serpent following him and steadily drawing closer, until the hunter remembered the warning of his friends and darted sidewise around the slope. Outdistancing his pursuer and continuing to the top, he saw the great serpent slowly making its way toward the summit.

The hunter thereupon hastened to the base of the mountain, set fire to the grass and leaves, and soon the flames crept up the slopes until they reached the top. In a short time the fire had surrounded the dread monster and it was burned to ashes.

Legend of Blood Mountain[6]

Blood Mountain, rising 4463 feet above sea level, is one of the Blue Ridge chain and stands on the boundary line between Union and Lumpkin counties in north Georgia, forming the divide between the headwaters of the Nottley and Chestatee rivers. It is two miles west of Neel's Gap on the Appalachian Trail and is the legendary home of the Nunnehi or Immortals, the people who live anywhere. They were a race of spirit people who lived in the highlands of the old Cherokee country and had many great dwellings, especially on the high bald peaks on which no timber grows.

These spirit people were invisible except when they wanted to be seen, and then they looked and spoke like other people. They were fond of music and dancing, and Indian hunters in the mountains would often hear the dance songs and the drums beating but were never able to find where the dance was being held. They were a friendly people and often brought lost hunters to their homes under the mountain, feeding and caring for them, finally guiding the lost ones back to their own homes. Many times when the Cherokees were hard-pressed by their enemies, the Nunnehi warriors are said to have come forth and saved them from defeat.

Once four Nunnehi women came to a dance at Nottley Town. They danced with the young men there, who thought they were visitors from another settlement. About midnight they left to go home and some men who had gone outside to cool off watched them go down the trail to the river ford, but when they reached the water's edge they disappeared, so the watchers knew they were Nunnehi.

Many tales have been told of these spirit folk by reputedly honest people among the Cherokees, and, according to them, there must have been many of the Nunnehi living in that neighborhood, because the drumming was heard in the high, bald peaks almost up to the time of the removal of the Cherokees.

Legend of Hiawassee[7]

The headwaters of the beautiful highland river of Hiawasee are in the southern part of Towns County in north Georgia, the river itself running north and west along the Blue Ridge, through North Carolina and into Tennessee, where it joins the Tennessee River. *Hiawassee* is an Indian word, variously interpreted as meaning "beautiful savannah" and "pretty fawn," the latter interpretation based on a legend of a sad Indian love.

During one of the frequent wars between the Cherokees and the Catawbas, a large town of the latter was captured by the Cherokees. Nottley, son of the Cherokee Chief, took for his prisoner Hiawasee, daughter of the Catawba chief.

He fell in love with his charming prisoner, and it was soon evident that she returned the love of this handsome warrior and daring horseman. Nottley had the innate sense of honor to feel that he should take Hiawassee back to her father and ask him for her hand in marriage. He knew that it would be a dangerous thing to do, and it was, for the proud Catawba chief lifted his war club, curled his lips in scorn and said, "The Catawbas drink the waters from the west; the Cherokees drink the waters from the east. When you find where these waters unite you may ask for the hand of the daughter of a Catawba chief."

Nottley was discouraged but he did not despair. Day after day he searched the mountains, hoping to find the place where the waters united. Resting one day on the ridge of a mountain, he saw two fawns and, quietly following them, saw them drink from a lake at the foot of the ridge. Observing closely, he saw that from the lake ran two streams in opposite directions, one east and one west. Springing up with the bound of a deer he cried "Hiawassee, Oh Hiawassee, I have found it!"

He hurried toward the wigwam of Hiawassee's father, but before he reached it she met him and he told her of his find. "My father will never let me marry the son of a hostile tribe," she said, but seeing her lover's downcast look she added, "I will fly with you to your mountain home," He joyfully replied, "Then we will drink together the water of that beautiful lake."

Nottley asked Hiawassee's father to consent to their marriage, but in a rage the old chieftain refused, saying that Nottley had deceived him in order to obtain his daughter's hand.

That night Pretty Fawn was missing. A search was made, but no trace of her could be found. Her father decided that Nottley was an honorable man and that he had indeed found the confluence of the waters.

The Indian story tellers say that the two can still be seen by the lake enjoying the place where the streams run both east and west.

The Legend of Nacoochee

In the upper part of White County lies the beautiful Nacoochee valley. It takes its name from Nacoochee, Evening Star, daughter of an Indian chief. She was said to be endowed by the Great Spirit with a strange and bewitching beauty. The whole tribe loved and worshipped her, and in doing so almost forgot to worship the Great Spirit, who made her.

But Nacoochee loved only Laceola, son of a hated rival chief, whom she had been meeting secretly in a beautiful valley where branches of muscadines with bunches of purple grapes and clematis vines with pure white flowers formed a bower. There the murmuring water was hurrying to join the Chattahoochee; truly this was an ideal place for them to dream of love! They met and vowed to live and die together.

The chieftain was told of these secret meetings and vowed vengeance on any of a hostile tribe who should aspire to take his daughter in marriage.

Nacoochee heard her father make the vow, but her love for Laceola was greater than her fear of her father, and his threats were disregarded. The lovers felt, however, that it was best to leave the village, and when it became known that Laceola had stolen their Evening Star the warriors hastened to overtake the escaping couple. They were quickly discovered and the warriors tried to kill Laceola, but Nacoochee, seeing the danger, sprang before him and received the arrow in her own breast. Laceola, realizing that she had died for him, made no further resistance and gladly mingled his blood with hers in death.

The two lovers were buried in one grave in the beautiful valley of Nacoochee, where a lofty mound marks their resting place. From the center of the mound there grew a lovely pine which proclaimed to the world that love like theirs could never die.

Legend of Yahula

Yahula Place on Yahoola Creek, ten miles north of Dahlonega, in Lumpkin County, Georgia, is the site of another legend of the Nunnehi, or immortal people.

Yahula was a prosperous stock trader among the Cherokees, and the sound of the bells hung around the necks of his ponies was heard on every mountain trail.

Once there was a great hunt in which Yahula took part, and after the hunt it was discovered that he was missing. All search for him proved futile.

Some time later he appeared at the home of his friends as

they were about to sit down to supper, but he refused to eat with them, saying that he had been found by the Nunnehi, and as he had partaken of their food, he could never again eat with his friends or stay with his own people. He must return to the Nunnehi.

Yahula often returned to visit his people, but their entreaties for him to remain with them must have angered the Nunnehi, for his visits finally ceased and he was never seen again.

Many of the older Cherokees who took part in the migration to the West claim to have heard the tinkle of his ponies' bells and the sound of his voice in song when they passed along the creek trail at night.

The Legend of the Cherokee Rose[8]

The Cherokees, who lived in what is now north Georgia, and the Seminoles in south Georgia and Florida, were bitter enemies. The Cherokees were ever hoping for the time when the Seminoles would all be scattered or killed. It happened in one of their frequent bitter fights that a young Seminole chief was taken captive and sentenced to death by the Cherokees. But he fell so seriously ill that his enemies decided to postpone his execution until he was somewhat restored to health.

As he lay ill the daughter of a Cherokee warrior became the nurse of the young chieftain. It was said that the smile of the Great Spirit was not more beautiful than she, who rivaled in grace the bounding fawn, and to whose beauty many a warrior of her tribe had done homage. It is thus no surprise that even as death stared at the young cheiftain, he fell in love with the warrior's daughter.

As he grew steadily better, the dark-eyed maiden urged him to flee. But he refused to go unless she would go with him. He preferred torture and death to the fate of living without her.

She finally consented, and at midnight they silently slipped away into the still darkness, guided only by the moon. But before going very far, she was overcome with remorse for deserting her own loved ones. Wishing to have some token of remembrance, she slipped back to her father's house. She plucked a branch from a trailing vine, and, as she journeyed with her lover to the land of the Seminoles, from time to time pressed it to her heart. She planted it at the door of her home and there it was an ever-blooming flower, snow white with a golden center, a daily reminder of her far-off Georgia home. Thus it was that the Cherokee Rose derived its name.

TALL TALES AND HUMOR

The Ribbon Around Her Neck

Once upon a time a man fell in love with a beautiful girl who wore a pink ribbon around her neck. "Why do you wear a pink ribbon around your neck?" he would ask, and she would only laugh lightly and answer with, "I'll tell you some day."

The couple was soon married, he in his white tie and tails and she in a beautiful white bridal gown of satin. A pearl tiara holding a lace veil was on her head, and around her neck was a pink ribbon. "Why do you wear a pink ribbon around your neck?" her husband asked when they were alone. "I'll tell you some day," she answered.

They were a very happily married couple. The man grew rich, he built a large house for his family, and he educated his children well. His wife bore seven children, four of them sons; cared for her home; and proved to be an extraordinary woman in all things. She still wore a pink ribbon around her neck.

"Now that we've been married so long, tell me why you wear a pink ribbon around your neck," he requested. His aging wife laughed gaily as she shrugged and said, "I'll tell you some day."

As all folk must, the couple grew old and the wife grew ill and was about to die. A doctor was called, but he could do nothing. After a long and happy life with her husband, her children, her house, and the pink ribbon around her neck, she was going to die. "You simply must tell me now," her husband said, "why you wear the pink ribbon around your neck." "Well, I suppose you are right," she answered. She reached up to her throat, untied the pink ribbon, jerked it away—and her head fell off.

The Ribbon Around Her Neck

The Huge Turnip[9]

A man fenced in his turnip patch. Then he sowed turnip seed in it. Only one seed sprouted. It grew to be so large a turnip that it lifted the fence corners.

The grower of this fabulous turnip entertained a visitor one night and challenged the traveler to "tell a bigger tale than that." In fact, if the visitor (upon going his way and returning) should bring back a tale that would cap his host's turnip tale, free entertainment both ways should go to him.

The traveler, at length returning, said,

"The biggest sight of my travel was five hundred men working on one pot. They were so far apart they couldn't hear each other's hammers."

The host inquired, "Why so big a pot?"

"To cook that turnip of yours."

He won his entertainment.

The Three Gapes[10]

There was an old country woman who lived all alone in her little cabin. Her nearest neighbors were the Gapes. The old woman had a habit of sitting up late at night and knitting—and gaping. She was also in the habit of talking to herself. The old lady always knit till she gaped three times; then she promptly retired.

The lazy Gape family, not understanding or appreciating her industry, were merely curious to know why she stayed up.

One of the Gape boys went over and hid in her chimney corner. While he was there, the old woman gaped, remarking to herself, so that he heard her,

"There's one gape."

Sure he had been detected in his eavesdropping, the boy ran home. He sent his brother back to pry into the secret. He got there in time to hear the old lady remark "that's the second gape," and he too ran home.

Old Man Gape appeared in the chimney corner.

"Here's the third and biggest gape of all, and I'm going to bed" was all the puzzled man could hear or learn.

The Spoilt Baby[11]

Once a Negro woman and her baby boarded a train to make a visit to some of her friends. Just after the woman sat down in the passenger coach, her baby began crying, and the crying got worse and worse. When the conductor came through the coach to collect the tickets, he noticed how the baby was crying and fretting and he said to the woman, "Ain't your baby spoilt?" She replied, "No, sur; no sur, they all smells dat way."

Plain Old Rheumatiz[12]

An Atlanta policeman tells the story of an old Negro man who persisted in crossing the streets anywhere but at the corners. One day the policeman said to the old man, "Here you are jay-walking again." The old Negro looked disgusted as he said: "Lis'en here Mistah Cop, I'se got respect for dat uniform dat's you'se wearing, but I jes' cain't say so much for dat brain you'se got under dat hat'; I jes' wants you to know dat I ain't got no jay walking, hit's jest plain old rheumatiz I'se got."

TALES OF PEOPLE AND THINGS

Old Town[13]

A tale is told of Old Town (Ogeechee Town), a settlement in Georgia, near Louisville, which antedates the settling of the state by Oglethorpe. Early in 1700 George Galphin, a South Carolina trader, crossed the Savannah River and established an Indian trading post at Ogeechee Town. On one of his visits to the post an Indian chief was attracted by the bright red coat he wore. Gazing covetously at the vivid garmet, the chief said to the trader, "Me had a dream."

"What did you dream?" asked Galphin.

"Me dream you give me that coat."

"You shall have it, said the wily trader, stripping off the crimson vestment.

At their next meeting, after the usual salutations, Galphin said to the Indian, "Chief, I had a dream."

"Ugh, said the chief, "What did you dream?"

"I dreamed that you gave me all the lands in the fork of the creek."

"Ugh," groaned the chief, "You have it, but we dream no more."

Thus Galphin acquired the land about Ogeechee Town, which was later called Old Town. Today, the name "Old Town" and the legend are all that remain of the once-prosperous trading post.

Sir Walter Raleigh

From an old tradition preserved by the Yamacraw Indians on the coast, Sir Walter Raleigh made a visit to Georgia on his western voyage to seek gold of the Orinoco, and talked with the red men. There is no documentary evidence to support this story, unless we connect it with the fact that Oglethorpe in ascending the Savannah River took with him Sir Walter Raleigh's journal. It was Oglethorpe's belief that Raleigh had visited this region and had landed at Yamacraw. Its latitude was well within range of his explorations, and there are landmarks tallying with his descriptive accounts.

Mordecai Sheftall

On July 11, 1733, a vessel bearing forty Hebrew colonists arrived at Savannah, but there was delay in admitting them into the province because of irregularity connected with their transportation. In time, they were sent back to England and then returned, but some of them migrated to Charleston and Philadelphia. Those who remained, mostly Portugese and Spanish Jews, proved fine colonists who gave generously to every cause of the colony. Mordecai Sheftall, born in Savannah in 1735, became one of the most zealous of the patriots in the Revolution. He was taken prisoner by the British and afterwards released on parole, at which time he was taken to Sunbury. There he saved the charter which stated that unless a meeting was held annually, the charter itself was to be forfeited. Mordecai Sheftall remembered the provision. With three of his fellow prisoners, who happened to be members of the Union Society, he managed to hold a meeting before the time expired. This took place under a tree which is said to have been the birthplace of the first Masonic Lodge organized in Georgia. The tree became known as the Charter Oak. When exchanged, Mordecai Sheftall was appointed a flag master to carry funds and provisions to the destitute inhabitants of Charleston, and he faithfully performed his trust.

Mammy's Clothes Basket

Augusta has her legend of Revolutionary days in the story of Stephen Heard, who was imprisoned in Fort Cornwallis (formerly Fort Augusta) and sentenced to be shot. During his incarceration Mammy Kate, an old Negro slave, was permitted to visit him twice each week to carry away and bring back his washing. The day before Heard was to be shot Mammy Kate visited him, and the story relates that Heard, a small man, was smuggled out of prison concealed in the basket of clothes which robust Mammy Kate bore proudly atop her head.

Legends of Nancy Hart, Georgia's Revolutionary Heroine[14]

While authentic information about Nancy Hart's early life is lacking, it is not difficult to gather tales and legends about her personal appearance or her heroic deeds during the years of the Revolutionary War. Nancy Hart held no claims to beauty. The homely giantess was over six feet tall, strong as a man, and cross-eyed. Though illiterate and unsophisticated, she was, nevertheless, a devoted patriot and lover of liberty. Nancy stands in the front rank of brave women in American and Georgia history.

Mammy Kate Delivers The Goods

Nancy Hart's maiden name was Morgan. She married Benjamin Hart, and they migrated from North Carolina to Georgia. The family into which she married was an aristocratic one. Her husband was a brother of the celebrated Thomas Hart of Kentucky. Their niece was the wife of Henry Clay. Thomas Hart Benton of Missouri was another noted member of that family. When the Revolutionary War broke out Nancy Hart and her husband and eight children were living in a log cabin in Elbert County, Georgia. Their home was located a few miles above the ford on Broad River, known as Fishdam Ford. She was as stout of speech as she was strong of body, and legend says that she swore like a trooper. She gloried in shooting and hanging British soldiers.

A favorite story concerns her slaying five Tories who invaded her cabin and demanded food. Nancy had just cooked a meal for her large family and it had been eaten. She told her uninvited enemies that she had only one tough gobbler left since they had shot her other wild turkeys. One of the British soldiers went out, shot the lone bird, and commanded her to cook it. While Nancy unwillingly prepared the food, she overheard one of the British soldiers say, "Well, we killed John Dooley." Dooley was a neighbor and a good friend of Nancy and Ben Hart. The news of his murder aroused Nancy to fury.

Her tactics changed. From a sullen, silent country woman, she now became a hospitable, witty hostess. She brought out plenty of food and drink. Her keen sense of humor was a potent as her corn whiskey. Under her gay mood and from too much to drink the soldiers grew boisterous and careless. As they grew more jubilant, Nancy plied them with more whiskey. Each time she passed their stacked guns, she slipped one through an opening in the wall. She had spirited away all but three when one of the men noticed the disappearance; all the soldiers rushed for their guns only to meet an enraged lioness of a woman. She sighted her musket on them and, in language plentifully sprinkled with oaths, dared them to move. Two Redcoats disregarding her warning made a plunge for their guns. Both fell to the floor with bullets in their hearts. Nancy held the others at bay until her husband arrived with reinforcements. Captain Hart intended to carry the Tories to camp as prisoners of war, but Nancy refused to let them go, saying, "These prisoners have surrendered to me. Shooting is too good for them. They shall hang." In a very short while, Tories were dangling in mid air, while the jubilant Nancy sang "Yankee Doodle."

In Elbert County, Rocky River empties into the Savannah River from the South Carolina side at Carter's Island. Carter's in turn is surrounded by a group of small islands. In Nancy Hart's day, these islands and marshes on both sides of the river were canebrakes. Upper Georgia was overrun with Tories, and the British commander was occupying Charleston, South Carolina. The soldiers stole cattle, horses, pigs, sheep, and goats and then turned them loose in the canebrakes. They intended to drive them into South Carolina for use by the British troops.

While the husbands and sons not serving in the army were stalking the forests and swamps trying to find their stolen property, Nancy Hart discovered that the canebrakes were teeming with these stolen animals. She promptly got in touch with the men and boys and led the way to the marshes, where they corralled the animals and drove them back home.

When the British guard arrived to drive their quarry to Charleston, they found no animals and none of the Tories who had been appointed to watch the animals. They found only Mrs. Hart and her small company of men and boys. In the fight that followed, the patriots took seventeen prisoners and the belligerent Nancy had the pleasure of assisting in their hanging.

Nancy Hart was once busy working in her cabin when she heard a horse galloping by; she looked out and saw a Liberty Boy riding for dear life. He entreated her to assist him, and she threw the door open saying, "Ride through the house into the swamp." When he had ridden through, she closed the door and awaited his pursuers. In a few moments the Tories dashed up and knocked loudly. Nancy feigned a limp and went to the door. She demanded, "What do you mean by coming here and bothering a poor crippled woman?"

"We're looking for a young boy on a horse. Have you seen him?"

"Was he on a sorrel horse?" asked Nancy.

"Yes. Where is he?"

"Well," she said deliberately and pointing in the opposite direction, "He turned off right yonder."

The British galloped away while the large, cross-eyed woman laughed to herself and swore at them.

Once while Nancy was boiling soap over a log fire in her kitchen she was telling her children the neighborhood news about the war. One of the children whispered to their mother that someone was peeping through a crack in the chimney. Outwardly Nancy paid no attention and talked on at a lively rate. While continuing her stories she was eyeing the crack in the chimney. Suddenly she dashed a ladle full of boiling soap through the crack. There was a roar of pain. She rushed out to find there a spying Tory neighbor. Before he could escape, she seized and bound him as her prisoner.

On her way to a grist mill one day, Nancy met a band of Tories with the British colors attached to their coats. They began to make fun of Mrs. Hart and then demanded to see her pass.

"Here is my pass," she replied defiantly, shaking her fist. "Touch me if you dare."

One of the party unhorsed her by jerking her foot up and striking the horse so that he started on a run for home. Nancy said nothing; she picked up the corn, put it over her shoulder and went on to the mill. A few days later the young man who had thrown her from her horse got a bullet through his shoulder as a warning not to play jokes on Nancy Hart.

Any time Georgia soldiers needed information Nancy was always ready to obtain it for them. General Benjamin Lincoln and General Henry "Light Horse Harry" Lee arrived from North

Carolina and were anxious to attack the British Army in and around Augusta, but they did not know the location of the enemy forces and the position of their artillery. Since all of their spies had been captured, they appealed to Nancy to undertake the dangerous mission. She outfitted herself with a basket of eggs and a bundle of housewares to sell to the British soldiers. Nancy returned and furnished the generals with all the data they needed, adding her own opinion as to the proper point of attack. The Patriot army moved upon the weak point she had indicated and promptly the British were forced to fall back behind the Augusta fortifications.

The Cherokee Alphabet

There is an interesting legend connected with the invention of the Cherokee alphabet by Sequoyah, whose English name was George Guess. As the story runs, Sequoyah overheard a discussion by three young braves concerning the superior talents of the white man. One of the Indians said that the whites had only to put talk on paper, send it any distance, however great, and it would be readily understood by the person receiving it. They all agreed that it was very strange indeed.

Sequoyah, after listening to the lengthy discourse, arose and exclaimed, "You are all fools; why, the thing is easy; I can do it myself." He immediately sat down and began to scratch strange marks on a rock at his feet. When he had finished he proceeded to translate the characters to the skeptical braves. The erstwhile inventor became very indignant at the derision cast upon him and vowed that he would complete a list of symbols whereby the Cherokees might be able to read and write a language of their own.

This Sequoyah finally succeeded in accomplishing about 1827, but it was many months before he could prevail upon his people to accept the alphabet. After its final adoption, the Bible was actually translated into the Cherokee tongue.

The Last Indian in the Okefenokee

The tribal laws of the Seminoles demanded absolute banishment as punishment for murder, and the last Indian in the swamp was probably one of those outcasts. When the tribe was moved further south into Florida, this Indian was left to spend his days alone in the Great Swamp. He was the only human being living in the area for many years.

He was often seen briefly by some of the white men who moved into the area when the Indians left, but no one ever got near enough to speak. The pioneers of the area were, of necessity, a tough lot, and when it was discovered that cattle sometimes disappeared from their meager herds, they formed a possee to search for the thief. The six men who penetrated the interior of the Great Swamp saw signs of the missing cattle which had probably been taken only to satisfy hunger. The Seminole knew nothing of white man's laws. The area had always been his, and any animals around were for his satisfaction.

When they were camping for the night the group was startled by a noise which proved to be the Indian trying to shoot the men with an ancient flint gun. The powder was too wet to fire, however, and the Seminole turned to run back into the darkness just as one of the white men fired his own rifle. The Indian was injured, but not badly.

The men had no means to convey him from the Swamp, and there was no law except their own; so they chose to execute him there, cutting his throat on what is called Billy's Island. It is still told, however, that any campers on the island should beware, for the ghost of the last Seminole still keeps watch over the place.

Legends of Robert Toombs[15]

General Robert Toombs, of Washington, Georgia, was noted for his wit as well as his eloquence. "I hope the Lord will let me go to Heaven as a gentleman," he used to say "I don't want to meet some of those Georgia politicians there. I'd like to associate with Socrates and Shakespeare."

In his arguments before the Supreme Court, General Toombs flayed the Reconstruction Governor, Bullock, and his legislature without mercy. He was informed that if he persisted he would be held for contempt. The next time he went before the court, he used severe language against the now-fugitive governor. "May it please your Honors," he said, "the Governor has now absconded. The little rule of the Court was doubtless intended to catch me. But in seeking to protect the powers that be, I presume that you did not intend to defend the powers that were."

Once asked what he thought of the North, he replied, "My opinion of the Yankees is apostolic. Alexander, the coopersmith, did me much evil. The Lord reward him according to his works."

A Federal officer standing nearby said, "Well, General, we whipped you, anyhow."

"No, replied Toombs, "we just wore ourselves out whipping you."

Many anecdotes are told in Wilkes County about the feud existing between its two distinguished sons, Alexander H. Stephens and Robert Toombs. On one occasion, the dialogue became so heated that Toombs, a gigantic man, shouted to the frail Stephens, "Why, you little runt, I could swallow you in two bites!"

"In that case" Stephens replied cooly, "you would have more brains in your stomach than you have in your head!"

On another occasion, when Stephens had concluded his famous speech opposing secession in 1860, General Toombs arose in the Georgia Legislature and said, "Fellow citizens, we have just heard a speech from one of the brightest intellects and one of the purest patriots in America. I move that this meeting now adjourn with three cheers for Alexander H. Stephens."

Afterwards General Toombs was complimented by an opponent on his handsome behavior on this occasion.

"Thank you," said the General, "I always behave myself at funerals."

When Horace Greeley was nominated for President in 1872, Alexander Stephens bitterly opposed his election and started a newspaper in Atlanta in order to defeat the ticket in Georgia. Mr. Stephens was not a businessman, and the venture soon failed. When the campaign was over, he felt honor-bound to give promissory notes to cover the loss, an amount which took his hard earnings for many months to come. In this, he was like his friend Abraham Lincoln, who voluntarily saddled himself with a debt not of his own making.

As soon as General Toombs learned of Mr. Stephens' action, he hurried to Atlanta, bought the notes for several thousand dollars, carried them to Mr. Stephens and tossed them in his lap. "Here, Aleck," he said, "are those notes you gave those Atlanta people. Use them to light the fire."

Henry Grady's Practical Joke

The famous orator and editor Henry W. Grady was fond of practical jokes. Once in his early years, when he was starting his newspaper career on a Rome, Georgia paper, *The Commercial*, he was sent to solicit an advertisement from an old merchant who, in refusing, treated Mr. Grady with such rudeness that the young man was determined to get even.

Returning to the office, he wrote an advertisement calling for cats of all kinds to be delivered to the merchant's store.

Of all things, the merchant hated cats. When a multitude of cats of all kinds descended on him, he was furious and bewildered.

Grady was on hand to watch the fun, looking very innocent, but he didn't deceive the old man who glared at him, saying, "Sir, you did this!"

"Yes, acknowledged the young editor, "you see it pays to advertise in the right paper."

The merchant was not appeased; his profanity was fervent. But after he calmed down, he realized the truth behind the joke. He sent Grady an advertisement and became one of the closest of Grady's friends, but he never forgot the cats and often recalled them with mirth.

Mittie Bulloch's Son Teddy[16]

In Roswell, 20 miles from Atlanta, stands the white-columned house where Theodore Roosevelt's mother, Martha Bulloch, was reared and married. Nearby is stately Barrington Hall, whose former owner, Mrs. Baker, was one of the bridesmaids at the Bulloch-Roosevelt wedding.

On a trip to Atlanta where he, as President of the United States, was greeted with an ovation and kept busy every hour, Theodore Roosevelt thought of his mother's home and of her girlhood friend. He sent Mrs. Baker a message that he would like to see her. But a President's request did not shake the lady's old-time conviction that a lady shouldn't call on a gentleman.

She sent the President word that she would receive him at three o'clock the next afternoon. Good naturedly, he cancelled engagements, deferred his leaving, and travelled twenty miles on a clay road to pay his respects to Mrs. Baker, who received him not as the President but as Mittie Bulloch's son, an act which delighted Mr. Roosevelt.

Mr. Robinson's Bad Loan

The late Frank M. Robinson, for many years secretary and treasurer of The Coca-Cola Company, enjoyed relating how he achieved financial independence.

Shortly after Reconstruction, Mr. Robinson and Asa C. Candler were two young pharmacists on small salaries. Out of his meager savings Mr. Candler bought the prescription for Coca-Cola, then called by another name. Mr. Robinson mixed the first prescription and renamed the drink Coca-Cola.

Having no money with which to buy ingredients and advertising, and knowing that Mr. Robinson had saved $250, Mr. Candler asked his friend to lend him the whole amount. Mr. Robinson parted with his savings, wondering if he would ever get it back, with money so scarce. Finally, unable to repay, Mr. Candler insisted on settling the debt with a large block of Coca-Cola shares. Mr. Robinson rebelled at this, since he had small faith in the drink, but he was obliged to take the stock. It made him a millionaire. In his later years, he always said that he was wealthy in spite of himself.

The General[17]

This fox was red, and he had one enormous club-foot which distinguished him from all other local foxes.

This particular fox was noted as the smartest, gamest, most cunning fox that ever lived in west Georgia. His club-foot made an impression in the sand and soft ground more than twice as large as an ordinary fox track. Besides, by the manner in which he led a pack of hounds, local sportsmen always knew when they had flushed the old master.

Big Tom Parsons, a great fox hunter, named this fox the "General," and the name stuck.

The General lived during the 1870's and spent his long life in the vicinity of Mount Sinai, a densely wooded, mountain-like hill which lies in southwest Talbot County, Georgia. In his day the General was chased by many a famous July and Redbone hound and by many packs of fine fox dogs, but no individual dog and no pack of dogs could ever run him down.

Judge Henry Willin, a neighbor of the General's, owned a very famous hound, a hound that once ran a red fox for thirty-six hours, followed it across the Chattahoochee River more than thirty miles from where the fox was flushed, and caught it! But this dog could not catch the General.

On different occassions famous hounds were brought in from Tennessee and Alabama to run the General, but like all other dogs that trailed him, the Old Magician outwitted them all. The General would always run, seven days in the week, if the hunters would bring on the dogs. He was a "dead-game" sport, as all admitted; but whenever the General decided to quit for the day, he would break for Sinai and there lose the dogs completely.

No one has ever known how or why this fox could baffle a pack of hounds at Sinai. His ability to throw the dogs off trail, and vanish without trace or scent—always, however, at Sinai, is still a mystery.

The theory advanced many years later by Uncle Sank Cartright, an ex-slave, was that for years prior to and during the career of the General, some people had operated an old fashioned ash hopper on the northern slope of Sinai (where they leached lye from wood ashes, with which to make soap), and the General had learned to go and dip his feet and roll his body in the lye-impregnated residue scattered thereabouts. This, according to Uncle Sank, killed the fox's scent and confused the hounds, and, of course, explained his elusiveness.

In his old age in 1878, much to the disgust and deep regret of every local sportsman, the General met an inglorious end. He had no apparent fear of men and would often show himself. And meeting him in the public road one day, a young man killed him with a shotgun, or as the fox hunters expressed it: "Murdered, in cold blood, the grandest, boldest and smartest fox that ever lived."

TALES OF THE SUPERNATURAL

Every old house in Georgia would blush with shame if it couldn't harbor at least one ghostly apparition. Add to those a varied array of ogres, witches, werewolves, swamp lights, graveyard haints, and mountain apparitions, and Georgia is crowded with its collection of the supernatural. "Red-head-and-bloody-bones," an ogre which feeds on children and dwells in abandoned wells, occasionally still prowls in the swamps, and demons sent from Satan still roam the piney woods.

Usually these emissaries of the Devil take cover when humans pass, but one man who had had a few drinks saw a haint when returning home. The story teller took very little notice of the spirit, however.

A Description of a "Haint"

"I met him in the pasture las' night as I'se gwine home. Of co'se I didn't take no time to take no special notice of 'im, but as I passed 'im I seed dat he had a long body, wid crooked hind legs dat was black, an' he had short yellow fore-legs. Also he smelt like a goat, his belly drag de ground, an' he had a double set of teeth in his mouth. He had big pop eyes, a short tail, an' a white star on his breast. On his back I seen a hump like a saddle, an' his breath was awful. Naw, sir, I didn't take up no time with dat haint. But I did see 'im lick out 'is tongue about a yard, an' his ears set on his head lak a dog's and one of his front tusks was broke down to about nine inches long. His head was as big as a bushel an' when he stomped, the earth shook. But, lak I said, I didn't take no special notice of 'im."

The Witch That Took Off Her Skin[18]

Once a man married a witch who went riding every night on a broomstick. The man, of course, didn't know this before he married her.

Now this man wasn't very smart, but he began suspecting something was wrong. If he woke up at night and reached over to where his wife was supposed to be sleeping, she wasn't there. So he went for a talk with his sister, who was a very smart woman.

"Sister," he said. "If I wake at night and reach over to the place where my wife is supposed to be sleeping, ain't she supposed to be there?"

"Sure, Brother," she answered.

"Well, Sister, a week ago I woke up and reached over to the place where she was supposed to be sleeping and she wasn't there, and then the night after that I reached over to the place where she was supposed to be sleeping and she wasn't there, and the night after that I reached over to the place where she was supposed to be sleeping and she wasn't there."

"Something is wrong," said the man's sister.

"What's wrong?" asked the man.

"That's what we gotta find out," said the sister.

"How we gonna do that?"

"Tonight you ain't gonna go to sleep. When you gits in bed don't you close both eyes. You just close the eye nearest her so that she'll think you're asleep. And when she gets out of bed you watch what she does."

The man did just as his sister suggested. About midnight his wife looked over at him, and seeing the eye nearer her closed, she got out of bed. Just about that time there was a tap at the window and the man's wife quickly shed her skin in the corner, grabbed a broomstick, and flew out the window to another witch that was waiting for her outside.

At dawn she came riding through the window, flew over to the corner where she had deposited her skin and said, "Skin, Skin, don't you know me?" And her skin jumped right on her. She quickly crawled back into bed and looked over at her husband to see if he were asleep. Well, she thought he was because the one eye which she could see was still closed.

"Something is wrong," thought the man, "and I must tell my sister about it." And he did.

"Why, now I know that's wrong," said his sister very wisely. "You done married a witch."

"A witch?" said the man. "Tell me about them."

"Well, a witch is a mean woman that rides animals and people while they're sleeping. Of course they rides without their skins; everybody knows that. About midnight every night they goes out hunting their prey for the night. Why, you yourself have been ridden by a witch at some time or other."

"No!"

"Yep," she answered knowingly. If you ever wake in the middle of the night in a sweat a witch has been riding you, and if you ever wake with a backache, she's been at it again. And people ain't all they ride. If you find your horse or mule in the morning with his mane tied in knots, they been riding him, too. They rides everything and everybody. A witch can even make a cow go dry by milking a towel in her kitchen." She paused a while to let it all sink in.

"They disturb everybody. Everybody, that is, that don't take precautions, like me."

"What kind of precautions, Sister?"

"Well, I keeps a sieve under my bed 'cause the witch has got to go in and out of every hole before she can ride you, and by that time it's morning anyway. But some people prefer to keep the Bible under their beds. The witch, she's got to read every chapter before she can ride you and that takes all night long.

Now tonight after your wife done gone riding, you get up and put salt and pepper all over her skin. That'll fix her good.

The man went home and did just what his sister had said.

About dawn the witch came in. She flew right down to the place where her skin had been shed.

"Skin, skin, don't you know me?" The skin didn't do nothing.

A little louder, "Skin, skin, don't you know me?" The skin never moved a bit.

She was mad now, so she grabbed that skin and started pulling it all over her, but the skin was hurting so bad it couldn't help her at all. And when she got it on, the salt and pepper burned her so bad she started yelling.

Now all this woke her husband.

"I know you're a witch," he said, "'Cause my sister told me so and she's smart like most women are."

At that the wife opened the window, dropped her skin again, and called out to her old hag friend to wait for her. She flew out the window and was never seen again.

The Playful Ghost[19]

The Surrency family had no enemies; their history had no ugly deeds or crimes to call for a nemesis. But in 1872 a ghost took up residence with the Surrencys, finally driving the family from their home. Macon, Atlanta, and Savannah newspapers sent reporters, and Henry Grady visited the scene, together with about 8,000 other visitors who came to see the poltergeist perform. The railroad ran special trains at tourist rates from Brunswick to the little South Georgia town near Jesup.

Among Mr. Surrency's seven children was a daughter of sixteen named Clem. From the time she was four or five she had a habit of often running to her mother, insisting that something was trying to scare her. She was highly nervous, and nothing the parents could say or do could persuade the child that what she thought she saw she had actually imagined. The poltergeist performed best when she was around.

The demonstrations started in the home when Mrs. Surrency

was sewing in her bedroom alone. The pitcher in the bowl on the washstand began rocking, lifted itself high in the air, and rested finally at her feet. Then it rose again and shattered itself violently on the floor. From that day the peace of the Surrency home was destroyed, never to be re-established.

Often when the family was at meals, milk, water, tea, coffee, or soup would be flung into a lap, and once the entire service was pulled from the table and then through an open window. Furniture moved from place to place; the clock seemed to enjoy spinning about from hour to hour so that it chimed constantly. Smoothing irons and bricks were hurled about the house.

At times the strange force showed a vein of humor. Mr. Surrency took some valuables out of the dwelling and put them into an outhouse to hide them from the destructive poltergeist. When he returned to the house he had hardly stepped inside the door before he heard a crash behind him. There in pieces were his valuables.

Among Mr. Surrency's possessions was an exceptionally handsome pair of cut-glass wine decanters, presented to him by a fishing and hunting club in Savannah. Fearing they would be broken, he buried them in the garden about two feet below the surface. Upon returning to the spot to see if they were still safe he found nothing but fragments of the decanters all over the area. Even the solid glass stoppers were broken.

Quite often the pillows and mattresses would be jerked off the beds and pitched across the rooms. Chairs, even big rockers, were thrown against walls, some miraculously undamaged. The poltergeist seemed to enjoy playing with Mrs. Surrency, for she could hardly even sew when it was performing. Her scissors, her thimble, or even the garment on which she was working, would rise in the air and drift as though carried by unseen hands.

One Sunday when the poltergeist was performing more sensationally than usual, a church-going visitor passed the word just as the service began. When he reported what he had seen the entire congregation left for Surrency.

The hospitality extended by Mr. Surrency during the time of this visitation cost him a great deal of money. Anyone who entered his home he accepted as a guest, and many of the visitors who came to see the performances of the poltergeist stayed for lunch.

Foster, the great medium and clairvoyant, visited the scene with some of his friends, remaining there a week. He reported that he had talked with the spirits, and they had simply replied that the entire family was exceptionally mediumistic and the spirits needed them to deliver their message to the world. The Surrencys had no faith in Foster and soon sent him packing.

In all these performances no one was hurt except on two occasions. Once, when Clem was alone she was struck on the arm by a falling chair but was only slightly bruised. The other incident was more serious. The oldest son in the family once glanced at his brother, who was reading across the room, just in time to warn him about the andiron which had just been thrown at him. The boy fell unconscious and bleeding. The next day the Surrencys moved from the house, never to return.

The fine old house stood deserted for a half century, and then it burned. But several old timers still insist that strange lights and unusual sounds still come from the vacant lot where the Surrency poltergeist played.

The Legend of Sinking Mountain[20]

Fishtrap Mountain is disappearing. A few decades ago this Northeast Georgia mountain raised its peak as high as any of its brothers, but now it cannot compete in height. Some old timers who live in the neighborhood can remember when the mountain soared its crest among others of the Blue Ridge foothills in that area northeast of Lakemont. Today the mountain has settled a great deal, losing so much of its altitude that it is commonly called Sinking Mountain.

Any stranger asking the reason for the mountain's extraordinary loss of height is told the legend of Sinking Mountain.

Grey Eagle, the chief of the Cherokees in that region of north Georgia, decided that he had given up to the invading white man as much land as he intended. For forty years he had fallen farther and farther back into the mountain areas until at last he had only one mountain and the valleys around it.

But still the white settlers pushed on. A family moved quite near on the South and began breaking land for spring planting.

On the North the hunters incessantly invaded the last of his sacred hunting grounds. There had never been bad blood between the white man and the red man here, but something had to be done.

"Call all the medicine men of the nation," he had commanded at the last campfire meeting of the Cherokee chiefs. From the area now known as western Carolina came old Arrowhead, wise and ancient in his wisdom of the medicine men, and from the western plains (now called Columbus) came Blue Star, an ancient Squaw, whose medicine-man father had flaunted tribal laws by teaching his daughter all his wonderful secrets. But once given, the gifts of the mountain gods cannot be recalled, and she sat with full strength in the circle of the medicine men. The young and hard Chicotee, from the land of the trembling earth, Okeefenokee, was there with herbs the others had never seen. In a few weeks the group was complete. They were fully prepared to hear the bidding of the greatest chief of the Cherokee nation.

Grey Eagle rose and began: "From the sea they came with their new civilization. They took our lands and ruined our hunting. They married our squaws, and even pushed us from the sea of plenty where the fish run. But this valley they will not take. Not without a price. You have been called together to form the most powerful of all groups. With your wisdom I command you to put on this mountain all the curses possible in order that we will never leave. If this mountain is not to be the Indian's, it is not to be anyone's. Put a curse on this mountain, therefore, that can never be broken. If this land is taken from the Indian, let it sink into the ground, where it will disappear forever."

The medicine men were needed. The mountain would surely disappear if ever the last of the Indians left this sacred mountain. Here they were to stay forever, and only at the risk of losing their lives would the white men push them out.

The incantations began. One medicine man beat on bones of a great sea turtle while chanting the curse of the water gods. Blue Star used her most powerful medicine, a watery substance filled with the liquids from the bellies of all the animals of the area. With it she sprinkled her own blood around the base of the mountain to mark off the red man's land. Wise old Green Arrow lay on his face in the sight of the sun god all day, uttering the oldest and most powerful incantations he had learned so long ago from his own father, who could remember when there were no white men in the Indian's country that the new settlers called Georgia.

The last action consisted of a blood sacrifice of a doe, an eagle, and a wild boar, all killed together to mark the end of the affair. But when the white men heard of the affair they were not impressed.

The settlers continued coming. They broke land and ruined the hunting areas, and finally their governors insisted that all the remainder of the tribe take the "Trail of Tears" to Oklahoma, where the red men were promised land which would be theirs forever. Chief Grey Eagle was among those who died on the long march, but his last reminder to the white guards was of the curse he had put on Sinking Mountain.

And slowly it sank. Some scientists who don't believe in curses insist that the mountain is sinking because of the natural washing that has opened vast caverns in the area where the last Indians once lived in caves.

But the oldest residents of the area say it isn't so. They point with satisfaction to the mountain that is sinking and tell of the curse of Grey Eagle as the reason for the apparent sinking of the mountain.

Georgia's Werewolf[21]

The only werewolf in Georgia's ghostlore is said to be buried in O'Neal's District in Talbot County. Some of the older citizens can tell the story of the old spinster who turned into a wolf at will to maraude among the sheep.

The whole county had always thought the oldest sister of the Burton family was a little odd, and there was talk among the slaves of seeing her wander among the graves in the grove nearby or of locking herself in her room for days without seeing anyone, but no one could put much trust in those old slave tales, especially when they concerned such a highly respectable family as the Burtons.

It was just about the time that the Burton spinster returned from her latest trip to Europe that the sheep of the farmers began to be attacked. Each night, in spite of the guards around, the maurauder would take his toll—never for food, but for the joy of killing. Several valuable sheep dogs were lost at the time, too. Although a few of the farmers in the area reported that they had seen the culprit and shot at it repeatedly, nothing seemed to fell it.

Its species was unknown. There were some grey wolves still in Georgia's forests at the time, but this animal's tracks were not those of the grey wolf. Nor were the unearthly moans of pleasure which it sent forth after a night of killing those of any known animal.

Traps were tried. More guards were placed over the sheep at night. New rifles were bought and professional hunters were engaged, but the traps remained empty. Although the hunters seemed to hit the animal, as evidenced by a few drops of blood on the ground, the depredations continued.

One farmer who had suffered more extensive losses than the others swore that he would kill the animal. To make doubly sure that he would be rid of it, he offered a $200 reward for its head. He was surprised when he received a note asking him to go to the farm of a new settler, a man who had but recently arrived from Bohemia. The writer was a thrifty, hard-working and religious man who was separated from the people of the valley by a language barrier.

"Back home in Bohemia, I remember we have this same trouble," the immigrant said to his visitor. "People lose their sheep for months until a very smart man nearby tell us of the werewolf legend of my people. The werewolf, he love to kill for the sake of killing, just to taste the blood; not for food. So we villagers did the same thing I am asking you to do. Here is my silver cross. Take it and melt it into the shape of a bullet. Give it to your best hunter for his rifle. It is the only way a werewolf can be stopped."

Jackson, one of the victimized farmers, was desperate enough to believe anything, even a crazy tale from a foreigner. The silver cross was melted down and fitted into his own rifle, and Jackson insisted that he himself would stand guard for a few nights.

He was not kept waiting long. On the second night of his vigil the marauder came to the flock he was guarding and began its nightly slaughter. Jackson took careful aim from an advantageous position and fired. The beast screamed, but not like an animal cry. Instead it was the sound of a woman's voice— piercing, desperate, and haunting. He hurried to the place and searched closely for the animal, but it was nowhere to be found. Instead, however, he found the left front foot of the beast, where the silver bullet had cleanly sliced it off. The slaughter stopped.

No one thought it strange that the Burton spinster now had a bandaged left arm; they assumed that she must have hurt it somewhere. It was not until years later that the town doctor revealed that on the very night of the shot he had bandaged the spinster's arm for what looked like the damage from a bullet which had taken off her entire hand and wrist.

The Ghost with a Headache[22]

A strange bit of legal procedure it was, and if it didn't appear in the court records of Richmond County for the summer of 1831, no one would put much credence in the story. But lawyers and judges are to be trusted, and a man was hanged because of it, so one must accept the testimony at face value.

Paul McKellam had regretted leaving the University of Georgia when his father died suddenly, but there was no one else to care for his mother, their plantation on the Savannah, and his two younger sisters. As time passed he seemed to be doing a good job, or at least everyone said so. He always had been a bit wild, but what young man wasn't? No doubt he'd marry soon, and, of course, he'd settle down then. Why, he had even set that old overseer Rand Folson straight a time or two, and right within hearing of the slaves. Perhaps his father had put up with Folson's bullying and surly ways because they had been together for over thirty years, but not young Paul. He was now boss, and it looked as if he might be hiring a new overseer soon.

The slaves particularly loved the handsome young master. Hadn't most of them seen him ride his first horse, fall off and get right back on! And didn't they remember telling him stories about how the rabbit lost his tail, and why the peacock struts about, and why the bear sleeps through the winter!

"The planting should be finished today," young Paul would suggest, and finished it would be, for the workers took great delight in pleasing their young master. But Rand Folson wasn't pleased in those days. Nor would he ever be. The care and cultivation of the plantation had been his responsibility for too many years. Now his discussions with the new master always ended in arguments.

So hard did young Paul McKellam work that he took for his bedroom the small store room adjoining the office to keep from waking the family when he was up late. One morning he did not appear to give his daily work instructions. Perhaps he had worked too late into the night and was sleeping. Or maybe he had stayed at the poker game over at the Randolph's house.

A look into his bedroom settled the matter, however. Paul was dead. The doctor who examined the body suggested several possibilities; heart attack, or perhaps a stroke, but he was puzzled, too. A young strong body like that would show signs of either cause of death. Young Paul was soon buried in the family plot near the house.

It was not until several days later that Mrs. McKellam recovered from her grief enough to come down for breakfast, but when she did she saw waiting for her Paul's mammy, now old and past working age, but still lively in mind.

"I'm sorry, Miz McKellam, but you gotta know dis! Yesterday while I was at de church prayin', I looked up at de altar and seen Marse Paul sittin' on de step a-holdin' his head like it hurt 'im. Something's wrong, Miz McKellam, and he ain't restin' in peace till it be righted!"

"Aunt Lila," I know how you feel," answered the mother, "but such stories don't help much. Now I forbid you to spread such things."

"Yes'm," she answered. And the matter was dropped for a while.

But Mrs. McKellam's day was again interrupted when late in the evening she had a request from Big Jim, Paul's personal house slave, to talk to her.

"I seen Marse Paul today," he said. "Out under the water oak, walking forth a-holding his head like it hurt. He looked right at me, and his face was drawn wid pain."

A week passed and the matter was forgotten. The overseer again began running the plantation by cruel and exacting methods.

Mrs. McKellam had another caller, a friend of long standing who was certainly neither imaginative nor given to tales told by slaves. Two of her own servants had insisted that she drive over to the McKellam plantation to see if anything was wrong. They had seen wandering around the fields a man who looked like young Paul, holding his head in pain and beckoning for someone to come to his aid.

This was too much. Mrs. McKellam consented to having the body exhumed. A closer search was made of it and there, hidden by the long locks of hair was a nail which had been driven into Paul's head. The key to the carpenter shop was held by only one man, the overseer. Rand Folson was arrested, and he confessed when the slaves began testifying. Court records record his hanging on August 11, 1831.

The wandering spirit of young Paul was never seen again on the plantation.

The Hitchhiking Ghost[23]

The age of the automobile has produced at least one ghost, Georgia's famous and lovely hitchhiker, one version of the most widely-told ghost story in America.

One rainy spring night a university student was driving from Athens to Atlanta when he was surprised to see, hitchhiking along the highway, a lovely young girl dressed in white lace. She quickly explained that she was trying to get home and asked if the driver could help her. Being assured that he certainly could, she got in and gave her address. Because she was drenched she insisted on sitting in the back seat, but she did accept his proffered coat. The downpour kept the young man's attention on the road, and there was little conversation. Upon arriving at the given address he turned around to find that the girl was gone, but the seat and floor were still wet.

Inquiring at the address he found that the girl had been dead several years, killed while driving home from her senior prom. On the anniversary of her death she is apparently allowed one more try at getting home. The mother of the girl expressed regret that her daughter might have caused him any trouble.

The student was quite dubious about the whole story until he decided to drive to the girl's grave on the following day. There hanging on her gravestone, and still a little damp, was his coat.

The Wickedest Man in the World[24]
(A Legend of Spanish Moss)

Once upon a time there lived along the Georgia coast a man feared by all his neighbors. He was so wicked that he scared children and tied tin cans to cats' tails; he beat his wives; and everybody said he was the meanest man in the whole world.

Why, this fellar was so mean that not even the Devil was meaner. And you know how the Devil likes mean people. This man would compliment the devil, and the devil would compliment him on his meanness.

Well, finally it came time for this man to die. But the Devil, knowing how much bad he was doing in the world, was reluctant to cut off all that sinning, and this man was doing a powerful lot of it. But one day after the wicked man had lived longer than 'most anybody, the Devil was 'most forced to come after him. Being so mean, the man recognized the Devil immediately.

"You ain't come after me, have you, Mr. Devil?" he asked.

"You're darn right. I shore am."

"Why, I'm ashamed of you, Mr. Devil. How come you want me when you know I does more evil than anybody in the world? Why I'm even meaner than you, and that's powerful mean. Everybody says so."

"Well, that's right. But you've done been here longer than what's 'lowed."

"Well, as a reward for my meanness, promise me that you'll let me stay a little while longer."

"I promise. But remember, you gotta be mean as you can."

"Oh, and one thing more. Since we're such good friends, why don't you just promise that 'fore you come after me next time, you'll send me a sign of some kind?"

"Why, I reckon that's all right. I'll promise. What kind of a sign does you want me to send you?"

"I don't really care, Mr. Devil! Long as it's something I can see or hear."

"All right. But you ain't got but a few more years 'fore I'll be coming back for you. I'll remember that sign—something you can see and something you can hear."

Well, the Devil left and the meanest man in the world was smiling to see him go. 'Cause he was not only meaner than the Devil, he was smarter, too. And he knew that as he was getting deaf and blind, when the Devil sent his sign the wickedest man in the world couldn't see or hear it.

Well, it worked out just the way the mean man thought. In a few years he was completely blind and couldn't see nothing and he couldn't hear nothing neither. Lighting struck with his name on it and thunder screamed his name.

The Devil couldn't keep his promise. And though he sent sign after sign, the meanest man could neither see nor hear them, so the Devil was obliged to leave him on earth, just like he'd promised.

Well, the old man grew older, but he couldn't die. After a while he couldn't talk. But still the old man lived, doing everything mean he could think of. Finally he got so mean that the people of the coastal towns wouldn't even speak to him. So he just wandered. He didn't have no food, so he grew thinner and thinner while his grey hair grew longer and longer. He wandered up the coast, getting thinner. And he wandered down the coast, his hair getting longer all the while. Finally he just vanished—he didn't die, mind you, 'cause he couldn't—he just sort of disappeared. All you could see of him was his long hair blowing all 'bout in the trees; and his hair blew 'bout so that it just grew fast there, and now most folks know it as Spanish Moss, but it ain't so; it's the hair of the meanest man in the world.

The Old Man's Mossy Beard

J a c k s o n b o r o:
The Town That Died of a Curse[25]

In the fall of 1830 Lorenzo Dow was travelling about the
hamlets of Georgia looking for sinful folks who needed to be
saved by his preaching. He should have been quite happy with
the little town of Jacksonboro, for it had the reputation of
being the roughest town on the Georgia frontier. Located near
Sylvania, one hundred miles upriver from Savannah, it was a
pioneer settlement hewn out of the Georgia pine wilderness. The
brawny lumbermen of the area made their living by felling the
great pines, nailing them together into crude rafts, and then
poling the clumsy flatboats down the swift, winding Savannah to
a market greedy for the hard-to-harvest crop.

When the men returned they were ready for what they
termed a little entertainment, which usually started with a visit
to Nell's Saloon (or maybe the White Elk, which was next door)
and ended with a street fight. A Georgia historian of 1829 says
that ". . . in the morning after the drunken frolics and fights,
you could see children picking up eyeballs in tea saucers! There
was so much gouging going on." Of course some people doubt
historians, but that's just what he said.

It was regrettable that Evangelist Dow entered town just as
the men were celebrating the naming of their hamlet as the
county seat. Dow was a strange sight with his long black hair
streaming down his back, his wild eyes that shown brighter
when he screamed at the top of his lungs to the drunken
revellers, "Repent, brothers, repent!"

The men were in no mood for repenting at the moment. I
suppose Dow didn't really know that, or perhaps he'd have
waited till another time to visit. You have to give him credit for
perseverance, however, for the little hunch-back preacher wasn't
satisfied with just telling the men to repent; he insisted on
overturning drinks and pushing the inebriates out of the saloon
into the streets to hear him. No wonder that when he rounded
up enough people for a congregation, he received a barrage of
rotten eggs and tomatoes instead of the strains of "In the Sweet
Bye and Bye."

Finally, the men could take no more of his preaching, and

several went for a rope to hang the screaming little evangelist. "String him up, and let's get back to the saloon," yelled Big Nell. She was echoed by persons expressing similar sentiments. They grabbed the little preacher and already had the rope around his neck when a shout of "Stop that!" was heard.

They stopped, because the man who shouted owned most of the land nearby. His name was Goodall, and while he had no particular interest in the wild preacher or his message, he did care for law. The rope was taken from Dow's neck and Goodall asked him to remain the night at his house on the edge of town where he would be safe. Besides, he felt a little sorry for the man. He had heard rumors from Massachusetts, where the little Methodist minister had started his ministry, that he intended to convert every sinner in every frontier village on the Eastern seaboard.

Now the first part is in doubt, but Dow's preaching did take him a long way—from Massachusetts to Western New York and Ohio, back to Virginia, through the Carolinas and down to Georgia, where he insisted he found the wickedest folk of all. Some said the little man was just plain crazy, but he had his followers, too. He had no money of his own, living entirely on the charity of those to whom he preached, depending upon them for the small amount of food, clothing and shelter he required. Sometimes he was forced to sell his horse, but then he'd walk for miles with his feet bound in rags until someone provided him with another animal.

He met a variety of receptions. On occasion he had been run out of town. In Charleston he was jailed for twenty-four hours and fined. In Savannah he preached on three occasions to vast crowds. However, never had he found men so sinful nor less ready to repent of their sins than in Jacksonboro.

The morning after his unexpected reprieve he returned to town and gathered a crowd around him.

"I hate to do this to you people, but it's been commanded," he shouted. "Since you wouldn't receive me I plan to shake the dust off my feet as I leave your town. The place will die, and with it, I hope some of your wickedness."

Laughter came from a few hecklers and soon spread among the crowd. The audience bent double with guffaws. Imagine that little runt cursing the promising town of Jacksonboro!

"Except for the Goodall home, of course," Dow corrected. "There I was received." And the little preacher got on his horse, rode to the edge of town, and as he shook his feet free of the dust of the village, he pronounced the curse of Sodom on its inhabitants.

No one thought anything odd when the first home burned that very night. After all, there were fires all the time. On the second day there was a small landslide on the mountain nearby, and this time two houses were completely covered by rocks and several villagers were killed.

This was only the beginning of the tragedies. During the next two years houses were destroyed by unexplained fires, damaged by mysterious winds which ripped off roofs, and battered by flash floods from the usually quiet creek. The market for pine dropped in Savannah, and the Legislature ordered that the county seat be moved to another town.

No one ever said it aloud, but they all knew. "Repent, repent," they kept hearing when the wind was strongest, and some unexplainable and seemingly supernatural event would occur, taking with it another of the structures of the place. Soon the remaining families began leaving, too. But the curse did not stop the rampaging accidents and by 1840 the town of Jacksonboro no longer existed.

Except for one house. If all these natural phenomena were merely the result of nature, then why does the Goodall home still stand? But there it is, even today. Not so beautiful as it used to be, but it is still there.

A visitor can look for miles around, however, and he won't find a nail or a board of what was once the thriving little village of Jacksonboro. Walk every foot of it, and there's not one other stick, stone, smidgen of glass to offer that anything was there. Just natural progress, the younger people say, but most of the old folk nod their heads and still believe that Jacksonboro vanished because of the curse of Lorenzo Dow.

S y l v i a t h e S n o o t y G h o s t[26]

Panola Hall, the white-columned home of Dr. and Mrs. Benjamin W. Hunt of Eatonton, was haunted during their lifetime by a lovely ghost whom Mrs. Hunt named Sylvia. The house was built in 1790 and the walls of solid masonry are twenty inches thick. Dr. Hunt was a scientist and farmer who moved his new bride into the house in 1876 and lived there for sixty years. When they arrived as a young couple, Sylvia was already there. She was a beautiful, hoop-skirted young woman, dressed in white and wearing a rose on her shoulder. The Hunts quickly accepted her as a member of the family. Although they often saw her as she climbed or descended the stairs, they never spoke of her to outsiders.

Sylvia was persistent enough to appear to many of the Hunts' friends, however. Once she was seen in the library by a group of people standing across the street. Dr. and Mrs. Hunt were in the living room; he was reading and she was doing needlepoint. Then a young woman appeared behind Dr. Hunt and looked over his shoulder. She stood there a long time, but the Hunts continued their evening activities. Later, when asked about their beautiful visitor, the Hunts were forced to admit that the group had seen Sylvia.

Once a house visitor encountered the young lady on the stairs, and Sylvia did not speak or nod. The Hunts had to explain that their home was haunted by a beautiful ghost.

Dr. and Mrs. Hunt felt very strongly about Sylvia, but some of their friends had reservations. Miss Bessie Butler was taking care of Mrs. Hunt in her last illness when she found occasion to enter the room called "Sylvia's Lair," then being used as a linen closet. Sylvia appeared in the corner and called, "Miss Bessie, Miss Bessie," but the nurse grew frightened and ran out. Dr. Hunt was angry because he felt Sylvia had a message for them.

Sylvia left the home after the Hunts died. *Panola Hall* is now a rooming house, and no one has seen Sylvia in years. Those who knew her best insist she has found more congenial surroundings.

A DICTIONARY OF GEORGIA GHOSTS

1. *The Ghost of Allatoona Pass*
The old Western and Atlantic Railroad passes about five feet

from the grave of a Confederate soldier who haunts the tracks near Marietta. While trying to cross enemy lines to return to his company, the soldier was shot. Since then his ghost has carried a lantern along the track looking for his comrades. Sometimes his dog runs in front of an engine, stopping only when the train passes the grave.

2.   *The Ghost Train of McDonough*

One of the most persistent of all ghosts in Georgia is not a person but a train which has been trying to arrive at its destination for half a century. In 1919, while approaching McDonough, the train was wrecked and all passengers and crewmen were killed. Since then the whistle blows, the engines roar, and the smoke rises in the air, but the train itself never reaches the little station.

3.   *Mary-de-Wander of St. Simons*

A beautiful indentured servant named Mary haunts a long road on the former Demere Plantation on St. Simons Island called *Mulberry Grove*. Because the master of the plantation forbade his son to marry the girl, the younger man angrily left the island during the famous hurricane of 1824. He was drowned before reaching the mainland. Mary heard the news and drowned herself in the haunted place now called Mary-de-Wander. Her spirit waits for the young man who will never return.

4.   *St. Simons Lighthouse*

One of the earliest lighthouse keepers on St. Simons Island was murdered there by an employee he had dismissed. The keeper still concerns himself about his duties, however, for his ghost returns on stormy nights to make sure the lights are burning to warn ships away from the shore.

5.   *Ghosts of Ebo Landing*

At Ebo Landing on St. Simons Island, where slave ships formerly discharged their human cargo, one of the last groups of captives brought to Georgia refused to submit to their masters. The first night on shore, led by their chief, the entire group committed suicide by marching into the sea while singing. On moonless nights they repeat the mass drowning amid the hanging moss and the water oaks.

6. *The Christ Church Cemetery Lighting*

On St. Simons Island old residents tell of a young wife who was afraid of sleeping alone. Her husband promised he would not let her sleep in the dark. He evidently remembers, even from their spirit world, for often a strange light has been seen illuminating her grave.

7. *The Hinesville Well*

A strange, sad parade often takes place around a well near Hinesville. Legend recalls that three girls were killed by their mad and frantic father, who heard mistakenly that there was a group of raping and marauding Yankees in the area. He chopped off the girls' heads and threw them in the well. Their apparitions now appear near the well, apparently searching for their lost heads.

8. *Cheever Home of Macon County*

This former hotel is haunted by a strange ghost who does not like to sleep alone. Several members of the family have felt the ghostly presence slide under the warm covers or sometimes turn in restless, ghostly sleep.

9. *Bonaventure Cemetery*

Nightly in Savannah's moss-hung Bonaventure Cemetery on the Thunderbolt River the strangest of all ghostly dramas takes place. Legend recalls that the fine old Tattnall plantation home which once stood there caught fire while the owner was entertaining at dinner. Knowing nothing could be done to save the house, Tattnall had his slaves remove the table and food to the garden. From there the dinner party watched the flames sweep away the magnificant mansion. Midnight visitors still claim to hear the ghostly laughing and talking of the family and their guests enjoying that famous meal.

10. *Ghost of Captain Flint*

The old Flint House, located at 26 East Broad Street, Savannah, is said to have been the house in which Captain Flint, a character from Robert Louis Stevenson's *Treasure Island*, passed his last days. The house has now become a famous restaurant, the Pirate's House. But the owners keep alive the old legend of Flint's haunting. "Darby, bring aft the rum," were the old villain's last words, and he must still be thirsty, for rumor has it that on stormy nights if one listens above the rumbling of the thunder, he can hear the old villain repeat this command.

11. *Fort Wimberly*

Five miles southwest of Savannah is the site of old Fort Wimberly, erected to protect the Wormsloe silk plantation from the Indians. If one listens he can often hear the ghostly sounds of muskets fired by Mary Jones, daughter of the original owner, Noble Jones. Once that intrepid female found herself alone at the Fort when the Indians staged an attack. She fired so rapidly that the Indians thought the place was well defended and quickly withdrew. Now from the spirit world Mary sometimes still defends her famous home.

12. *Renee Rondolia*

When Savannah was a village Renee Rondolia was born to good parents but grew into a sadistic monster. He was killed by an angry mob of Savannahans who refused to allow his body holy burial and instead consigned it to a brick tomb in the East Side Marshes. He still haunts the area, looking for his victims.

13. *Augusta's Haunted Pillar*

Situated on the corner of Broad and Center Streets in Augusta is a haunted pillar, on which at one time was the bloody handprint of a slave. This is the sole remaining pillar of the old market house which was destroyed by a tornado in 1888. A preacher of that era had predicted such a fate as punishment for the wickedness of the town. Whoever shall remove the one remaining pillar will be stricken with instant death, according to the curse. So today the old pillar stands unmolested on a prominent business corner of the town.

14. *Augusta's Dueling Ghosts*

At the old dueling ground situated at Sand Bar Ferry, located just three miles below the city of Augusta on the banks of the Savannah, late-night visitors are often rewarded with the sounds of the "affairs of honor" which were staged there. In stormy weather with bright lightning, one can sometimes see the flashing blades of duelists and hear the accompanying clashes of steel.

15. *Greene Street House in Augusta*

In a beautiful old home on lower Greene Street remain distinct saber cuts in the smooth stair rail just outside the ballroom at the top of the house. These are said to have been put there in the Provost Marshal days just after the Civil War. The Union Provost, hearing of the presence of some Confederate officers who refused to take the oath of allegiance, sent a squad of soldiers to arrest them. The members of the guard forced their way inside and encountered the Confederates on the stairs. A fight ensued in which at least two persons were killed. The saber marks on the stair rail bear mute evidence of the struggle. A constant dripping which plumbers are unable to locate is said to be the drops of blood of the Confederates, whose spirits still wander about the place.

16. *Augusta's White House*

Augusta's most famous haunted house is the old McKay's Trading Post, now remodeled and called the *White House*. During the Revolution a British colonel had thirteen Georgia patriots hanged in the house in order that he might see them from his sick bed there. The patriots take their revenge with ghostly groans and shadows on the old staircase.

17. *Elberton's Haunted Mill*

An old cotton mill in Elberton was haunted for years by a former female mill worker who always appeared in the distance hurrying from one frame to another. She was seen only when a mill employee was about to die.

18. *Elberton's Devil's Foot*

Some of the older people of Elberton can show a visitor the footprint of the devil clearly imprinted in a rock near the town. Because the print leads away from the town it is explained that the devil left, never to return, and that's why the people are so extraordinarily good.

19. *Milledgeville's Scott House*

In Milledgeville Miss Katherine Scott lives in a house formerly owned by a man whom the residents of the town always called the meanest man in the world. His evil deeds are legion, but his most notorious act occurred with his own son. The boy was home from college during a smallpox epidemic when he caught the dread infection. The father refused to fetch the doctor for the boy, insisting that he was not really sick. The father's ghostly penance is a frequent re-enactment of the boy's death as it occurs in his father's arms on the stairs of the old home.

20. *The Homestead in Milledgeville*

The Homestead in Milledgeville is haunted by a little old lady who sometimes flits between the boxwood hedges at dusk. She is a faithful ghost who followed the Williams family from Wales to New England and finally to Georgia.

21. *T. R. R. Cobb House in Athens*

Teaching nuns now occupy Athens' T. R. R. Cobb house on Prince Avenue. Before their coming, however, the ghost of an old gentleman wearing a gay dressing gown was often seen walking down the stairway and sitting before a fire in the drawing room.

22. *Lustrat House in Athens*

Major Charles Morris, A Civil War hero and Professor of *Belles Lettres* at the University of Georgia, liked to keep warm. For years his spirit has been said to wander around his old home on the University of Georgia campus—making fires in the fireplaces, stoking them, and then sitting before them in cozy contentment.

23. *Howell Cobb House in Athens*

The handsome columned house behind Emanuel Episcopal Church in Athens, which was one of several built for General Howell Cobb, is haunted by the ghost of Mary Thomas Safford. This tragic woman committed suicide after the birth of her child, and for more than one hundred years her ghost has returned whenever there is an infant in the house.

24. *John B. Cobb House in Athens*

The John B. Cobb House in Athens is haunted by at least three spirits, but they never seem to meet each other. Before leaving for war a young Confederate officer was married, then called quickly away before the marriage could be consummated. Often he returns, looking for the love of which he was deprived by a quick battlefield death in Virginia. Although they never seem to meet, his wife too wanders about the house. And neither of them bumps into the Negro slave who was left in charge when the boy she had reared went off to fight the Yankees.

25. *Jefferson Lamar Home in Athens*

During the celebration following the marriage of Jefferson Lamar, a Civil War colonel and a member of one of Georgia's oldest families, the newly-installed gas lights went out, leaving complete darkness. One of the family servants immediately saved the party by lighting fires in all the fireplaces. In the years following the servant's death, whenever the house had lighting problems, the ghost of the old servant returned, trying again to light the house for the wedding festivities.

26. *Crystal Lake*

The devil has a winter home in south Georgia. Near Ocilla, in Turner County, he spends much time at Crystal Lake. He plays often in the lakes in the area, particularly Lake Ross, which he drains whenever there is a drought.

27. *Hawthorne House*

The sad ghost of an infant haunts the old Hawthorne House near Cairo, Georgia. Legend tells of a destitute mother who killed her child there, and now the baby cries alone from the haunted corner.

28. *Means House in Oxford*
The Means House in Oxford, *Orna Villa,* is haunted by several of the family's ancestors. The house was built around 1820 and the history of the family tells of brother Toby who was buried out West but whose spirit cannot rest until his body returns to Georgia.

29. *Weather Prophet House*
A few years ago at Lincolnton, Georgia, a house suddenly became a weather prophet. Preceding a rain, a damp spot would appear in several places on the wallpaper, and noises of dripping water could be heard throughout the place just before a storm.

30. *Worth County's Indian Ghost*
The White man's action in the removal of the Indians is not easily forgotten in Worth County. There the spirit of an Indian squaw who hanged herself rather than embark on the Trail of Tears continually makes the sacrifice as a reminder of her people's suffering.

31. *Waleska's Howling Woman*
The traveler on an old dirt road leading out of Waleska comes around a curve and into a wooded glen before he hears a ghost, which often wails plaintively in the night. Some people have even heard the howls from the church nearby. It was in the same glen that an early settler was scalped and then dragged dying up the hill. She relives her agony now for night travelers in the place.

32. *Sneed-Wardlow House of Macon County*
A wide carriage drive around the Sneed-Wardlow house has long since been removed, much to the disappointment of a ghostly carriage which often still rides the old road on dark nights.

33. *McAllister House of Savannah*

The McAllister House of Savannah has now been torn down, but it was haunted for half a century by a spirit thought by many to be that of Mrs. George W. McAllister, who died in New York in 1856. The hauntings ceased when Mrs. McAllister's body was returned to Savannah for burial in Laurel Grove Cemetery.

34. *DuBose House of Wilkes County*

In a lovely old three-story house on the southeastern edge of Washington in Wilkes County, the DuBose home was haunted by Miss Mary Ann Pettus, who became such a member of the family that they reserved for her a small rocking chair near the fire. Sitting there in black with her hair smoothed down, she would rock contentedly both day and night. Miss Pettus haunted the house until she was literally crowded out when it was made into a hospital.

35. *Polly Barclay's Meadow*

Washington's most tragic ghost is the beautiful Polly Barclay, the first woman to be hanged in Georgia. She haunts the meadow west of the Pembroke Pope home, where her execution took place. Polly was convicted on the testimony of a boy who was visiting her home on that night. He swore that when a vehicle was heard entering the yard, she insisted her husband get out and investigate, 'though he was reluctant to do so. On opening the door he was shot dead, and Polly was accused of collaborating with the murderer. Though she protested her innocence to the end, and no one ever accused her of firing the fatal shot, she was convicted. So positive was Polly that this sentence would never be carried out that on the day for the hanging she arrayed herself in her finest garments and went smiling to the scaffold. After this dark event in the history of Wilkes County boys and girls for a hundred years would hide their eyes and run by the meadow where Polly was hanged to keep from seeing the lovely, sad soman wringing her hands and crying softly in the distance.

36. *Randolph House in Washington*

Miss Marcia Randolph, a direct descendent of Pocohantas, and one of Washington's earliest settlers, still haunts the stately old Randolph home in the eastern part of town. Later residents have often seen her wandering through the garden or the high-ceilinged rooms of the old mansion.

37. *Toombs Home in Washington*

Washington's most romantic wraith is the lovely bride in trailing white wedding garments and misty veil who on moonlight nights haunts the grove surrounding the Gabriel Toombs home on the town's main street. The ghost has been identified as Miss Sarah Hillhouse, the daughter of the state's first woman editor, who was married in the house more than one hundred and fifty years ago.

38. *Georgia's Haunted Castle*

A magnificent old Gothic structure now reduced to ruins rests on a hillside outside Rome. It is the castle of Godfrey Barnsley, an English aristocrat who made a vast fortune in cotton and ordered the twenty-six room estate to be built on ten thousand acres of land in north Georgia. The gardens were planted with trees imported from throughout the world, but the interior was still incomplete in 1861 when the workmen put down their tools and took up arms. Godfrey lost his fortune with the war, but his ghost still hammers in a part of the old house. It is said he cannot rest until his mansion is finished. A cycle of family misfortune was climaxed in the house in 1935 when a great-grandson of the builder murdered his own brother there.

39. *Ghost of Joel Cloud*

The Cloud place in McDuffie County is guarded still by Joel Cloud, who built his house in 1830. Upon his death he left it to his son, who discovered $40,000 worth of gold and a note which suggested that more treasure was hidden in the garden. If so, it was never found. Joel Cloud is said to still ride around the estate on his white horse, determined that only one of his descendants discovers the hidden gold.

40. *St. Elmo's Fire*

In most of the swamps of Georgia a swamp gas called St. Elmo's Fire, Will-o-the-Wisp, or Jack-o-Lantern appears as a light in the distance moving into the swamp. Strangers often insist it is a ghost haunting the place. The light disappears as one approaches, however.

41. *The Haunted Kolb Farm*

When a Cobb County man named Kolb was called for duty in the Georgia militia during the Civil War, four of his slaves attempted to escape to Northern Virginia. They were caught and returned, and the residents of the area insisted that they be executed as an example to other slaves who might be considering similar action. They met their fate on August 26, 1863.

Today the old Kolb farm is a part of Kennesaw National Park, and all visitors to it must walk past a gnarled oak tree near the site of the old house. If they listen carefully at night they may hear the cries of the four slaves, and sometimes the four figures may be seen dangling amid the leaves and moss.

42. *St. Mary's Headless Ghost*

For many years a headless apparition frightened guests at the old St. Mary's Hotel. It was the ghost of a man who was beheaded there during the Revolution and who was said to return to look for his lost cranium.

43. *Cumberland Island Carriage Ghost*

On Cumberland Island the residents of the grand old *Dungeness* mansion often heard a spectral carriage racing up the driveway. It is said that long ago a carriage filled with guests was wrecked while en route to a party at the house and that since then they have been frantically trying to arrive at the scene of festivities.

44. *Midway Church Graveyard*

When the Midway Church Cemetery wall was being built just after the Revolution, a fight between two of the workers resulted in the death of one. His body was quickly buried under a section of the wall. Because the wall kept cracking in that place the area was finally dug and the skeleton of the victim discovered. The ghost refuses to allow the place to be repaired, however, and the wall always cracks and crumbles in the same place.

45. *Crooked River State Park Ghost*

A Spanish priest still walks around his old mission wall at Crooked River State park near Kingsland. He may be listening to the spectral, mournful chants of slaves buried in the old plantation graveyard nearby.

46. *Jefferson's Christmas Dog*

When Uncle Jim Randolph drank a bit too much at Christmas time, he and his little dog would wander around Jefferson throwing coins for the children of the town. Now whenever a child hears the ghostly bark of the dog near Christmas, he can find a coin nearby.

47. *McDuffie's Quaker Ghost*

The Quakers came to McDuffie County in 1768 and left in 1805, but they left behind the ghost of the Little Quaker, a woman who nursed Revolutionary War wounded in the *Old Rock House*. She still flits about, carrying a candle to show any soldiers the way to her hospital.

SOURCES

1. Georgia's Indian lore was first published by the U. S. Bureau of Ethnology in 1900 in James Mooney's *Myths of the Cherokees.* Some of the stories collected by the field workers are clearly adaptations of that material. The Mooney book is not generally available, however, so we are including some of those tales.
2. Field Worker: Olin Sneed. 1937
3. Field Worker: Olin Sneed. 1937
4. Informant: Mrs. Joe Thornton. Indian Springs resident. Field Worker: Henrietta Carlisle.
5. Field Worker: Nan Bagby Stephens. 1938
6. Field Worker: George C. Ward. 1937
7. Field Worker: Martha G. Bell, 1937
8. Field Worker: Martha G. Bell, 1937

9. Informant: H. H. Doogan. Field Worker: Swilling. Elliijay, 1936.
10. Informant: H. H. Doogan. Field Worker: Swilling. Elliijay, 1936.
11. Informant: Miss Geneva Roper and Mrs. Bess Hasty. Field Worker: Swilling. Dec., 1936.
12. Field Worker: Phillips. Atlanta, 1936.
13. The first four short tales were submitted by Field Worker: Nan Bagby Stephens.
14. Field Worker: George C. Ward.
15. Field Worker: Nan Bagby Stephens.
16. Field Worker: Nan Bagby Stephens.
17. Field Worker: J. R. Jones. Talbot County, 1936
18. Field Worker: Maude Barragan. Augusta, 1937. Rewritten by the editors.
19. Field Worker: Olin Sneed.
20. Field Worker: Olin Sneed.
21. Field Worker: J. R. Jones. Talbot County, 1936.
22. Field Worker: Louise Oliphant. Augusta, 1937.
23. This is America's most ubiquitous ghost. It was submitted in four manuscripts. Taken here from Field Worker: George C. Ward.
24. Notation across manuscript reads "A Georgia coastal legend." Rewritten by editors.
25. Submitted in 1962 by a University of Georgia student. Rewritten by the editors.
26. Field Worker: Harriett Hallsworth. Athens, 1938.

CHAPTER II

C O N J U R E

I'm going to pizen you, I'm going to pizen you.
I'm jes' sick an' tired of de way you do.
I'm going to sprinkle spider legs roun'd yo' bed.
An' when you wake up in de mornin' you'll fin'
yourself dead.[1]

The black art of conjuring, still practiced in some rural areas of Georgia, seems to be vanishing from the state. The last conjure woman either of the editors knew died a few years ago, and John the Conqueror root can no longer be purchased in the grocery stores of Georgia's major cities. Devil's Snuff also has disappeared.

Conjuring, that strange black magic which combines diverse elements of African voodooism, American superstitions, traditional medical remedies, Christianity, Mohammedanism, and individual imagination, was a lively and sometimes profitable part of both rural and urban life in Georgia for more than two centuries. Conjure, sometimes used synonymously with voodoo (or hoodoo, as it was more often called in Georgia) came to America through the slaves from the Ewe-speaking tribes of West Africa where snake worship still exists. The magic rites of the python deity migrated with the Negro to Haiti and then to the mainland, centering around New Orleans. The religion gradually lost its origins but retained its magic and mystery and spread over the South.

In Georgia conjure practice quickly followed the slaves. The plantation owner naturally protected his property by forbidding physical violence among the Negroes. The slaves, therefore, turned for redress to witchcraft or conjure. The latter usually was practiced by a fellow slave living on the same or on a neighboring plantation. The conjure doctor had remedies for all

66

the troublesome aspects of life, including an unreturned love or an active enemy. He had love potions, magic concoctions for revenge or finding hidden treasures, and foul-tasting medicine for inducing sleep or for protection against the "evil eye."

With the end of slavery the conjure practitioner became even more important. In every community after the Civil War a conjure worker, root doctor, hoodoo man, or guffer-man (the names vary but their functions remain the same) became a noted and sometimes rich community figure. Aunt Pickeye of Augusta used to drive over the town in a rickety wagon filled with swill tubs. She claimed to be the seventh daughter of a seventh daughter and to have been born with a caul over her head, both signs of great power. Henrietta Hamfidite of Columbus supported a large family by selling her conjure medicine; she insisted she was the first to discover the powers of "ground puppies," a dried powder made from insects.[2] In the 1930's Professor Redmond of Savannah called himself "The Mysterious Man of New Orleans" and was so successful that he set up office hours and saw clients only from 9:00 a.m. to 9:00 p.m. An extant advertisement, dated 1936, reveals that in those Depressions years his exotic concoctions were relatively expensive.

> *Vang Vang Oil — 50 cents. put a few drops on your clothing and it will bring you luck.*
> *Black Cat Sachet Powder — $1.00. Put a little in a small cloth bag and wear it on your person. Brings luck and love to wearers in money matters and wins in all kinds of games whether it be in numbers, cards or dice.*
> *Lucky Mojoe Sweetheart Drops of Love — 50 cents. Use on clothing or handkerchief, a little on the eyebrows. This brings good luck in love and business. The fragrant sweet smell of this perfume will hold the loved one enchanted.*
> *Lucky Mojoe 7-11 Holy Oil — 25 cents. Priests before the birth of Christ anointed themselves with this oil. Brings success in undertakings and keeps away evil spirits. Put a few drops in your dresser and in your place of business or even on your money. It ensures success.*

The strength of the conjure spell depended primarily on the conjurer.[3] A red-eyed man or woman was easily recognized as a powerful conjurer, and anyone with one blue and one black eye was particularly gifted. The greatest conjure gift of all, however, went to the blue-gummed man or woman; no power on earth could weaken his spells. To be "strong in hand" was to possess great strength of will—the most important requisite of the conjurer. To obtain this strength, one must first drink a pint of whiskey into which had been put some black bark gathered from two small saplings which rubbed together in the wind. The higher a person climbed for the bark, the higher his rank in the conjuring arts.

INGREDIENTS FOR CONJURE[5]

Dried frog, lizard, snake etc.

> Dry and then pulverize the skins of these reptiles. The victim must be tricked into drinking a liquid with the powder in it. The animals will begin growing in his body.

Five-finger grass.

> This plant has a leaf divided into five segments. When hung in the house over the bedstead it will bring restful sleep and ward off any evil that any five fingers can bring about.

Lucky hand root

> This root resembles a hand, brings luck, and wards off evil.

Adam root.

> Spidery-looking root found in swamps. Adam root is single, Adam-and-Eve root a double root, Adam-and-Eve-and-the-children root is a double root with tentacles. Remarkably good luck charm. Wear the double root to win and hold a husband or sweetheart. Others will attract love, money, and success.

High John, the Conqueror root.

> Brings good luck. A person carrying this will never be without money. Supposed to win for you in games and love, drive off evil influences, and ward off bad luck.

LUCKY HAND ROOT

FIVE FINGER GRASS

DEVIL SNUFF

GRAVEYARD DIRT

BONE OF BLACK CAT

DRIED LIZARD

Ingredients For Conjure

Devil's snuff.

A large mushroom filled with gray powder. This toadstool is the Devil's snuff-box, and must be used in conjunction with other conjure elements to obtain power.

Devil's shoe string.

A long and slender root resembling a shoe string. If the root is placed around a baby's neck it will drive away evil spirits. It brings luck in money matters. Cut root into small pieces, put camphor or whiskey on it, and rub it on your hands; it will give you control over any woman. Rub inside of your hands with it and the back of the hands with devil's snuff, and grab your enemy by the arm when he comes for you; he will be blinded. Carry a bit in your pocket and no snake will bite you.

Graveyard dirt.

To be effective it must be procured from the coffin of a dead person in the waste of the moon, at midnight. A silver coin should be left on the grave to keep the spirit from bothering you. Rub it on your hands and you can conjure a person by shaking hands with him. Sprinkle it under his house or about his yard. That person becomes sleepy and gradually wastes away, or he leaves town.

Salt

A shoe filled with salt and then burned will call luck to you every time. Tied into your skirt it will make a gossip's teeth ache if she speaks evil of you. When thrown into an enemy's tracks it will keep him from returning.

Rattlesnake master.

A long root pulled at right angles to the moon. Put into a bottle, tell it what you want, cork tightly, place in a secret compartment, and it will accomplish your wish. Has very strong vibrations.

Ground puppies.

A tiny worm with horns which breeds in rotten wood. Dry and grind to powder. Makes powerful charms. Drop into the path of the person to be conjured.

Dragon's blood.

Red root fibers crushed for multi-purpose conjuring and protection.

Wild wonder root.

> Use for treasure hunts.

Ruler root

> Bury in your yard to keep things in your favor.

Conjure bag.

> A cloth bag to be worn about one's neck. Usually made from an old tobacco sack. Must be filled by a conjurer with various conjure elements to protect the wearer.

Dried breast bone of frog.

> Carry it in the pocket for good luck.

Lodestone.

> For wishing and love potions.

Black Cat's bone.

> The most powerful conjure charm of all. Anything can be obtained from the bone or ashes. The preparation, however, must be done with care. Following is a personal account from an eye witness:

HOW TO PREPARE A BLACK CAT'S BONE[6]

"You goes out in de valley in de woods an' you takes a live black cat dat ain't got a spot of white on him, an' you throws him in a pot of boiling water. Man, dat cat almost tear dat pot up tryin' to get out. You boils him till he gits done all to pieces an' den you takes all de bones an' throws dem in de creek an' de one dat floats up de creek is de one to use. You takes dis bone an' draws it through your teeth an' gits all de meat off, an' den you can take dat home an' do all kinds of magic. You can talk to folks an' dey can't see you. You can even disappear an' come right back. It takes a good 'un fer dat. While you'se boilin' de cat de thunder an' lightnin' look like it goin' tear up de face of de earth. You can even see de wind like a red blaze of fire."

"I knowed a boy who had de ashes of a black cat. He say dat he burned a black cat an' dat de night he burned 'im about twelve o'clock he could feel his soul hit de bottom-mos' part of hell. You see you has to sell yo' soul to de devil to git dis bone an' use it. One day de sheriff wuz after dis boy and while we wuz all sittin' on de top of de steps he spied de sheriff. When de sheriff come up he wuz gone an' after de sheriff left he wuz jus' sittin' there jus' where he wuz before de sheriff come up. I asked 'im where he went, an' he said nowhere, dat he had a black cat's bone an' nobody couldn't do nuthin' to him."

CONJURE SPELLS

For an aphrodisiac, combine rabbit tobacco, sage, ginger, wahoo bark, and the root of a chinaberry tree.

A common kitchen conjure can be done by sprinkling some salt and pepper 'round someone, and it'll bust their brains out.

For a love conjure, take some of the hair of the person you want and tie it in a sack with some of your own. If a woman does this she'll have to wear the sack with the hair tied to her garter. A man wears it in his pocket.

To make someone move, get some graveyard dust. Best to reach way down in a grave and get the red dirt and sprinkle it 'round the door of the person you want moved. He can't stay there after that.

To cause your enemy to have a headache, split a nut he has touched into two parts. To crush the nut will induce a bursting head pain and drive the victim to the point of madness.

Get the hair-ball of a sheep or cow which the butcher finds when he slaughters the animals and hide it under an enemy's doorstep to work evil.

To keep your man home, take some salt and pepper and sprinkle it up and down the steps. Then take a plain eating fork and stick it under the door steps, and he will stay home until you remove the fork.

To make a gambler lose all his money, stand behind the man or woman and sprinkle a little salt on his neck. From that moment on he will not win.

Make a love potion by drying and pulverizing the bodies of nine honey bees, caught on the ninth day of May, divided into nine equal parts with one part given in a drink to the one desired.

To run a person crazy, take a strand of his hair and nail it to a tree.

To hurt an enemy, write his name on a piece of paper and put it in a dead bird's mouth and let it dry up. This will bring him bad luck.

To hold a man, get some fishbait worms and boil them and strain the water. Then put in a spoonful of lard and boil some more. Then, wet the bottom of his drawers with the water, or his stomach, and they ain't nothing he can do. He won't never fool with any woman but you.

Easiest way to hold a man is to get a piece of thread out of his drawers and keep it. Then he can't get away long as you don't lose the thread.

To keep your wife from flirting around, take a persimmon sprout about six inches long and bury it under the doorstep while her flirting spell is on.

To drive your rival out of the country, take a limb from a poplar tree that has been struck by lightning and tie a dogwood sprout to it with a raw thread from a feed sack, and measure your rival's track with the sticks, measuring the same track nine times. Then bury the sticks where the rival will walk over them, and in nine days after he walks over the sticks he will walk to another country.

To make a woman drown herself, get a piece of her underwear, turn it inside out, bury it at midnight, and put a brick over it.

To bring good luck to a house, put guinea-pepper leaves in the scrubbing water and plant a guinea-pepper plant in the yard.

To punish an enemy, plant nine needles in an object and slip it under the house right under the head of the bed. They will cause nine pains to the person sleeping directly above them.

To make a woman drop dead, take nine hairs out of the tip of a black cat's tail, nine hairs from a hog's snout, nine hairs from a horse's tail and nine hairs from a black cow (don't make no difference what part) and mix 'em all with gunpowder into a ball. Then you say "East, West, South, North," and you call out her name three times and throw the conjure ball in the air. It'll sail like a kite and blow up and when the blue smoke comes out of it, she'll drop dead—no matter if she's gone all the way to Savannah.

Blindness is produced by the conjurer taking a frog and drying it, then making it into a powder which is mixed with salt, and sprinkling it in the hat of the person to be conjured. When the person sweats and the sweat runs down the face, blindness will result.

To conjure a well, throw into the well some graveyard dirt, an old pipe of a conjure doctor, and some devil's snuff.

To make a person leave town, get some dirt out of one of his tracks, sew it up in a sack, and throw it in running water. The person will keep going as long as the water runs.

To make a person travel, take a hair out of his head and put it in a live fish's mouth. Then throw the fish back into the water. The person will travel as long as the fish swims.

Take heads of scorpions, ground-puppy, toad-frog, or dried snake, pound them till fine, add to water or food. The varmints when taken into the stomach become alive and slowly devour the victim, unless he can get the conjure off.

If anybody come to your house and you don't want them there, when they leave you take some salt and throws it at them and they won't ever come back.

If you're having a fight and hold a can of any kind to the mouth of your opponent, you will catch his breath and cast an evil spell on him. He will have severe cramping pains.

PROTECTION AGAINST CONJURE

If you think you've been conjured take a little bit of rattlesnake master root and chew it up. When you spit it out, it breaks the spell because most conjures contain the root.

A lucky stone carried in the pocket attracts forces of good, keeps away forces of evil. Your enemy cannot fix you if you carry it.

Place a broomstick over the kitchen door to keep out conjure witches. They ride the broom instead of the householder.

A bracelet of dimes, worn around the ankles or neck, will protect you against conjure.

Sprinkle the doors of your house with chamber lye mixed with salt to keep the house clear of conjuring.

The buckeye will keep away conjure if it is kept shining.

Carry in your pocket (for strong protection against conjure) the left foot of a rabbit in a graveyard.

Place an X on your Bible, sleep on it, and it will protect you against witches and conjuring.

Put red pepper in your shoes to prevent conjure.

Fish bone will pick up the conjure if you have swelling from the spell.

To cast off a conjure against her baby, a mother must rise from her bed on the third day after the birth and walk around the house three times with a part of the hem of her skirt tucked into the neck of her dress.

A conjure bag prepared by a conjure doctor, filled with bits of frog skin, powdered blood, strands of human hair, and special roots, will protect you against any kinds of conjure for a year.

If you find a conjure bag in your yard, pick it up with two sticks, but don't look at it. Then throw the two sticks and the bag into the fire. Place the ashes in moving water.

To know when you have been tricked, wear around your belly or your ankle a dime on which either the number three or the number seven appears twice. When it turns black you will know somebody is trying to work a trick on you and you can go to a conjure woman and git it untricked.

Take two pods of pepper and one tablespoon of salt and put them in your right shoe; take one pod of pepper and one tablespoon of sulphur and one of salt and put them in your left shoe. Then whenever you walk over any conjure balls, bad luck plants, buried needles, powders, *etc.*, your feet will burn and warn you. If the conjuration is very bad, sometimes the sole will burn right off your shoe. But you will know somebody is after you and go and get untricked.

S O U R C E S

1. Informant: Mrs. Julia Rush, ex-slave. Atlanta. Field Worker: Edwin Driskell. 1937.
2. Informant: Mrs. Ellis Strickland, ex-slave. 1936.
3. Informant: Mrs. Julia Rush, ex-slave. Atlanta. Field Worker: Edwin Driskell 1937.
4. Informant: Hattie Taylor, ex-slave. Columbus. Field Worker: J. R. Jones. 1937.
5. Informant: Mrs. Emily Thompson, ex-slave. Atlanta. Field Worker: Edwin Driskell. May, 1937. Informant: Celestine Avery, ex-slave. Atlanta. Field Worker: Lillian Milner. Nov., 1936.
6. Informant: Celestine Avery, ex-slave. Atlanta. Field Worker: Lillian Milner. Nov., 1936.

CHAPTER III

CONJURE TALES

The Turtle in His Throat[1]

"Once a man named John tried to go with a girl but her step-pa, Willie, run him away from the house just like he might be a dog, so John made it up in his mind to conjure Willie. He went to the spring and planted somethin' in the mouth of it, and when Willie went there the next day to get a drink he got the stuff in the water. A little while after he drunk the water he started gettin' sick. He tried to stay up but every day he got wuss and wuss 'til he got flat down in bed.

"In a few days somethin' started growin' in his throat. Every time they tried to give him soup or anythin' to eat, somethin' would come crawlin' up in his throat and choke him. That was what he had drunk in the spring, and he couldn't eat nothing' or drink nothin'. Finally he got so bad off he claimed somethin' was chokin' him to death, and so his wife sont off and got a fortune teller. This fortune teller said it was a turtle in his throat. He 'scribed the man that had conjured Willie but everybody knowed John had done it 'fore the fortune teller told us. It warn't long after that 'fore Willie was dead. That turtle come up in his throat and choked him to death.

"Some folk don't believe me, but I ain't tellin' no tale 'bout it. I've asked root workers to tell me how they does these things, and one told me that it was easy for folks to put snakes, frogs, turtles, spiders, or most anythin' that you couldn't live with crawlin and eatin' on the inside of you. He said these things was killed and put up to dry and then beat up into dust like. If any of this dust is put in somethin' you have to eat or drink, these things will come alive like they was eggs hatchin' in you. Then the more they grow, the wuss off you git."

Frogs in His Stomach[2]

"I know you don't know how folks can really conjure you. I didn't at one time, but I sho' learnt. Everytime somebody gets sick it ain't natchel sickness. I have seed folks die with what the doctors called consumption, and yet they didn't have it. I have seed people die with heart trouble, and they didn't have it. Folks is havin' more strokes now than ever but they ain't natchel. I have seed folks fixed so they would bellow like a cow when they die, and I have seed 'em fixed so you have to tie them down in bed to die. I've got so I hardly trust anybody."

"My aunt's son had took a girl away from another man who was going with her too. As soon as this man heard they was going to marry, he started studyin' some way to stop it. So he went to a root worker and got somethin' and then went to this girl's house one night when he knew my cousin was there. Finally when he got ready to leave, he was smart enough to get my cousin to take a drink with him.

"That next mornin' the boy was feelin' a little bad, but he never paid too much 'tention to it. Next day he felt a little wuss, and everyday from then on he felt wuss and wuss 'til he got too sick to stay up. One day a old lady who lived next door told us to try a root worker who lived on Jones Street. This man came and told us what was wrong, but said us had waited too long to send for him. He give us somethin' to relieve the boy of his misery. Us kept givin' this to him 'til he finally got up. Course he warn't well by no means and this medicine didn't help his stomach. His stomach got so big everybody would ask what was wrong. He told everybody that asked him and some who didn't ask him 'bout the frogs in his stomach. The bigger these frogs got, the weaker he got.

"After he had been sick 'bout four months and the frogs had got to be a pretty good size, you could hear 'em holler everytime he opened his mouth. He got to the place where he wouldn't talk much on account of this. His stomach stuck out so far, he looked like he weighed 250 pounds.

"After those frogs started hollerin' in him, he lived 'bout three weeks, and 'fore he died you could see the frogs jumpin' 'bout in him and you could even feel 'em.

A Conjure Woman Mixes Her Evil Brew

"T'ain't no need talkin'; folks can do anythin' to you they wants to. They can run you crazy or they can kill you. Don't you one time believe that every pore pusson they had in the 'sylum is just natchelly crazy. Some was run crazy on account of people not likin' 'em, some 'cause they was gettin' 'long a little too good. Every time a pusson jumps in the river don't think he was just tryin' to kill hisself; most times he just didn't know what he was doin'."

L u c i n d a[3]

"When it comes to conjuration, don't nobody know more 'bout that, and there ain't nobody had as much of it done to 'em as I have. I know nobody could stand what I have stood. The first I knowed 'bout conjuration was when a woman named Lucinda hurt my sister. She was always a 'big me,' and her chillun was better than anybody else's. Well her oldest child got pregnant and that worried Lucinda nearly to death. She thought everybody she seed was talkin' 'bout her child. One day she passed my sister and another woman standing on the street laughin' and talkin'. Lucinda was so worried 'bout her daughter she thought they was laughin' at her. She got so mad she cussed 'em out right there and told 'em their 'turn was in the mill.' My sister called the other woman in the house and shut the door to keep from listenin' at her. That made it wuss.

"'Bout three weeks later my sister started complainin'. Us had two or three doctors with her, but none of 'em done her any good. The more doctors us got the wuss she got. Finally all the doctors give her up and told us there warn't nothin' they could do. After she had been sick 'bout two months she told us 'bout a strange man comin' to her house a few days 'fore she took sick. She said he had been there three or four times. She 'membered it when he came back after she took sick and offered to do somethin' for her. The doctors hadn't done her no good and she was just 'bout to let him doctor on her when this woman that was with her the day Lucinda cussed 'em out told her he was Lucinda's great-uncle. She said that everybody called him the greatest root worker in South Carolina. Then my sister thought 'bout how this man had come to her house and asked for water every time. He wouldn't ever let her get the water for him; he always went to the pump and got it hisself. After he had pumped it off real cool he would always offer to get a bucket full for her. She didn't think nothin' 'bout it and she would let him fill her bucket. That's how he got her.

"She stayed sick a long time and Mamie stayed by her bed 'til she died. I noticed Mamie wipin' her mouth every few minutes, so one day I asked her what did she keep wipin' from my sister's mouth. She told me it wasn't nothin' but spit. But I had got very anxious to know so I stood by her head myself. Finally I seed what it was. Small spiders came crawlin' out of her mouth and nose. Mamie thought it would skeer me; that's why she didn't want me to know.

"That happened on Tuesday and that Friday when she died a small snake came out of her forehead and stood straight up and stuck his tongue out at us. A old man who was sittin' there with us caught the snake, put him in a bottle, and kept him 'bout two weeks before he died.

"Lucinda went a long time, but when she fell she sho' fell hard. She almost went crazy. She got so bad off 'til nobody couldn't even go in her house. Everybody said she was reapin' what she sowed. She wouldn't even let her own chillun come in the house. After she got so sick she couldn't get off the bed she would cuss 'em and yell to the top of her voice 'til they left. Nobody didn't feel sorry for her 'cause they knowed she had done too much devilment.

"Just 'fore she died, Lucinda was so sick and everybody was talkin' 'bout it was such a shame for her to have to stay there by herself that her youngest daughter and her husband went to live with her. Her daughter was 'fraid to go by herself. When she died you could stand in the street and hear her cussin' and yellin'. She kept sayin', 'Take 'em off me, I ain't done nothin' to 'em. Tell 'em I didn't hurt 'em, don't let 'em kill me.' And all of a sudden she would start cussin' God and anybody she could think of. When she died it took four men to hold her down in the bed.

"I've been sick so much 'til I can look at other folks when they're sick and tell if its natural sickness or not. Once I seed my face always looked like dirty dish water grease was on it every mornin' 'fore I washed it. Then after I washed it in the places where the grease was would be places that looked like fish scales. Then these places would turn into sores. I went to three doctors and every one of 'em said it was poison grease on my face. I knowed I hadn't put no kind of grease on it, so I couldn't see where it was comin' from. Every time I told my husband 'bout it he got mad, but I never paid too much 'tention to that. Then one day I was tellin' a friend of mine 'bout it, and she told me my husband must be doin' it. I wondered why he would do such things and she said he was just 'bout jealous of me.

"The last doctor I went to give me somethin' to put on my face and it really cleared the sores up. But I noticed my husband when my face got clear and he really looked mad. He started grumblin' 'bout every little thing, right or wrong. Then one day he brought me a black hen for dinner. My mind told me not to eat the chicken so I told him I wanted to keep the hen and he got mad 'bout that. 'Bout two or three days later I noticed a big knot on the side of the chicken's head an it bursted inside of that same week. The chicked started drooping 'round and in a week's time that chicken was dead. You see that chicken was poison.

"After that my husband got so fussy I had to start sleepin' in another room. I was still sick, so one day he brought me some medicine he said he got from Dr. Traylor. I tried to take a dose 'cause I knowed if it was from Dr. Traylor it was all right, but that medicine burnt me just like lye. I didn't even try to take no more of it. I got some medicine from the doctor myself and put it in the bottom of the sideboard. I took 'bout three doses out of it and it was doing me good, but when I started to take the fourth dose it had lye in it and I had to throw it away. I went and had the doctor to give me another bottle and I caught myself hidin' it, but after I took 'bout six doses, lye was put in it. Then one day a friend of mine, who come from my husband's home town, told me he was a root worker and she thought I already knowed it. Well I knowed then how he could find my medicine everytime I hid it. You see he didn't have to do nothin' but run his cards. From then on I carried my medicine 'round in my apron pocket.

"I started sleepin' in the kitchen on a cot 'cause his mother was usin' the other room and I didn't want to sleep with her. Late at night he would come to the window and blow somethin' in there to make me feel real bad. Things can be blowed through the key hole too. I know 'cause I have had it done to me. This kept up for 'bout a year and five or six months. Then 'cause he seed he couldn't do just what he wanted to, he told me to git out. I went 'cause I thought that might help me to git out of my misery. But it didn't 'cause he came where I was every night. He never did try to come in, but us would hear somebody stumblin' in the yard and whenever us looked out to see who it was us always found it was him. Us told him that us seed him out there, but he always denied it. He does it right now or sometimes he gets other root workers to do it for him. Whenever I go out in the yard my feet always feel like they are twistin' over and I can't stop 'em; my legs and knees feel like somethin' is drawin' 'em, and my head starts swimmin'. I know what's wrong; it just what he had put down for me.

"When I git up in the mornin' I always have to put sulphur and salt and pepper in my shoes to keep down the devilment he puts out for me. A man who can do that kind of work give me somethin' to help me, but I was s'posed to go back in six months and I ain't been back. That's why it's started worryin' me agin."

The Soda Conjure[4]

"In olden days folks knowed 'bout conjuration and root-workin' just lak dey does now, but dere warn't nearly as much of it goin' on den. More peoples had 'ligion den, and dey had to serve God; dey didn't have time to serve de devil lak folks does now.

"Now, you can't stop a pusson's chile if you see him doin' wrong in de street, you can't run nobody's chickens out of your own garden, and you sho' better not speak too friendly to nobody's husband or wife. If you don't believe me just try, and I bet somebody will soon have you rollin' in pains. You don't have to do nothin' to 'em; just make 'em mad. Dat's what happened to me.

"I has always loved chillun and wouldn't do nothin' to hurt one for nothin'. But you don't have to hurt one, 'cause I know I didn't hurt any. I just tried to keep 'em from hurtin' one another. You knows how bad chillun is 'specially when a crowd of 'em gits together. Well one day some of 'em wuz on dey way home from school. I think dey must have started fussin' and fightin' at school, 'cause I wuz comin' from de store and seed four or five of 'em waitin' wid sticks and rocks. I started to say somethin' to 'em den, but dey warn't doin' nothin' but standin' dar. 'Bout ten minutes later another crowd come out of de street just above my house, and when dese other chillun seed 'em, dey broke out and run to ketch 'em. Dey caught 'em just below my house and started fightin'. I hated to see 'em hurt one another, so I went out and stopped 'em. But when I got out dar, one of de chillun had been hit on de nose and it had started bleedin'.

"I don't know what de chile told his ma when he got home, but dat night she came to see me. She wuz good and mad when she got dar. I didn't know what wuz wrong 'cause I hadn't done nothin' to her chile, but she cussed me for everything she could think of. She said I held her chile so dat de other one could beat him just 'cause hers wuz dark and de other one wuz light. She said she knowed all 'bout it and she wuz goin' to git me if it wuz de last thing she done. I tried to s'plain to her, but she wouldn't listen.

"I never paid no 'tention to what she said 'bout gittin' me. When she said it, I thought she meant to lay fer me and jump on me, but I warn't thinkin' 'bout her doin' dat. Well I wuz wrong; she had somethin' diffunt in mind. At de time she started workin' at me I had fergot all 'bout it. Den one day she stopped and talked wid me just lak nothin' hadn't happened. She done dis two or three times and I thought she had fergot 'bout de fight de chillun had. Den one day she come to my house and stayed a long time. 'Fore she got ready to leave, she axed me to give her some soda, said her stomach wuz hurtin'. I didn't think nothin' 'bout it and brought her de whole box to git some out of. After I give her de box, den she wanted a glass of water. She said she had et somethin' and it didn't digest. Atter she took de soda she didn't stay long.

"She sho' wuz smart, and I didn't have de least idea what she wuz up to. I wuz really glad of her friendship and thought she meant it, but I soon found out better. It wuz nearly two weeks later 'fore I felt the 'fects of it, and den I didn't think 'bout her. I thought I wuz just natchally sick. I went to de clinic 'til I got down in bed so I couldn't go. Den I had de doctors to come see me, but I didn't git no better. Ma had to come down here from de country to wait on me, but she had to go back home sometimes. One evenin' when she come back to Augusta, de man who brought her come in to see how I was gittin' 'long. Just as soon as he come in and talked wid me a little while he told my ma and husband dat no reg'lar doctor wouldn't never git me up 'cause dey didn't know how to doctor on me for my trouble. He said he knowed a little somethin' 'bout my trouble, but I had gone too far for him, and 'sides he really didn't do dat kind of work. He said he knowed a man who wuz good at cases like mine, and would send him to me if I wanted him to. My husband told him to send the man right away.

"Dat Monday mornin' my husband stayed home from wuk to hear what dis man had to say. He come 'bout twelve o'clock. I hadn't never seed him before, but soon after dat I found out dat nearly everybody in Augusta knowed him. Dey call him Dr. Buzzard. But jus' as soon as he walked in de house he started tellin' me 'bout de fuss I had had wid a woman, told me how she had been comin' to my house lately and told me dat she wuz de cause of me bein' in de fix I wuz in. When he axed me if I had loaned her anythin' out of my house I told him I hadn't. He kept axin' diffunt question 'bout what she had done when she wuz at my house. I couldn't think of one single thing, but he told me she had got me right dar in my own house, and dat she had fixed it in somethin' I had loaned her or somethin' she had got a chance to git to. I didn't think 'bout de soda 'til he started namin' some things dat folks could easily git you in. When he named soda dat's when I thought 'bout it, and told him just what happened. He said dat wuz zackly de way she had got me, she had put somethin' in de box of soda.

"My husband axed him how could she git me in de soda when us both had been eatin' de same things and it didn't git him. Dr. Buzzard told him dat wuz de diffunce in conjuration and pizenin'. If it had been pizenin' she put in de soda if would have got us both; but she warn't mad wid him, she just wanted to git me. He said when somethin' is fixed for one pusson, ten or twelve kin eat some of de same thing but it won't hurt nobody but de one it's fixed for.

"Dr. Buzzard treated me a good while, and he finally got me up. He had to give me somethin' to take 'cause she had got it in me, but he said, if she hadn't got it inside of me he wouldn't have to give me nothin' to take. If it hadn't been for him I would have been dead a long time ago for nothin' cept her meanness. And every since den I don't never trust nobody wid nothin' I got to eat."

The Mean Sisters[5]

"Don't mention root-workers or conjurers to me! I would rather have a lion or anythin' like dat after me 'cause I could run in a house or somethin' and git out of their way, but you can't git out of de way of a root-worker. You kin leave town if you wants to and they kin even make you come back, or if you are here they kin run you away. I's had plenty of trouble wid 'em, and anybody who knows me kin tell you how I's suffered.

"My biggest enemy is dead now, and de truth is, I's glad of it. Dat woman give me more trouble than you think any person could stand. Dese sisters always went for bad, and thought everybody was skeered of 'em. Dey had a habit of goin' to anybody dey didn't like and beatin' 'em. There's a family here in town now that reminds me of 'em. Dey git together and go 'bout jumpin' on men or women. Course dey'll go alone when dey go to whip a woman, unless she's supposed to be real bad.

"One day, one of these sisters jumped on my cousin, and when they started fussin', before they started fightin', my cousin's little boy come runnin' to my house for me. Just as soon as he told me what was wrong I jumped right out and went over there. When I got there they was fightin' and this other woman had my cousin down. Just as she started to kick her I snatched her back and tole her I thought she had done enough, and it wuz best for her to be on her way home or wherever she wuz goin'. Dis made her mad and she told me she didn't have to go home if she didn't want to, but of course since I wanted to be a bully for me to make her go. I told her I warn't a bully and didn't go for one, but at de same time I warn't 'fraid of dem who did go for bullies.

"Anyhow, she argued 'round 'til us got in it. I ain't a pusson who gits into fights and I don't want to be bothered wid folks who do, but I wuz glad to whup one of dem bullies. And I knowed dey couldn't whup me. I whupped her good, and when she found out she couldn't whup me she went flyin' to get one of her sisters. I knowed she wuz comin' so I waited right dar for her. Her sister come, but she didn't come back wid her.

"De sister argued a long time, and when she found out I warn't afraid of her she cooled down, but she told me dat I would hear from her again. I told her dat anytime she got ready to come back to come on and I would be glad to meet her. Dis happened in March and dat same year in October I went to pick cotton out in de country a little piece. She met me one evenin' when I wuz on my way home. As soon as I seed her I knowed she had some devilment in her head.

"When she met me she wuz ridin' a bicycle and she run right into me. I moved out of de way and kept on walkin'. She ketched up wid me and axed me if I wuz skerred 'cause I wuz out in de country by myself. I told her I warn't, but I kept walkin', and I suppose she thought 'cause I wouldn't stop I wuz afraid. She got off her bicycle and told me she wuz ready to finish de fight her sister had started, but I still kept walkin'. Den she ketched me by my hair and told me not to walk off from her when she wuz talkin', and dat started de fight. I don't know how long us fit dar, but I know I whupped her 'til she axed me to let her go.

"Atter dat she started workin' roots at me, and at first she almost got me. She knowed she couldn't whup me fair fist, but she thought she could git me down by workin' roots at me. Whenever she got ready to throw at me she would send most anybody to my house lake dey wanted to sell somethin' or wanted to find out somethin'. She had two or three ways to git up to me, and everytime somebody come to my house for her, I sho' could feel it.

"Den one day a old lady wuz at my house and I told her 'bout how dese people always come to my house, and how I always felt when dey left. You see I didn't know who they was coming there for 'til after they left and I would git sick. But dis old lady tole me to git some sulphur, red pepper, and salt, mix 'em together wid just a drop of kerosene, and whenever I thought somebody had come dar wid somethin' lak dat just to put dis stuff anywhar in de house and light it, let it burn real slow and if de pusson wuz really bringin' somethin' dar to hurt me I could tell 't 'cause dey would soon leave. Dis stuff would run 'em away, and would kill whatever dey had brought dar, too.

"I found dis to be true, and sometimes I even tried to keep de people longer, but I never wuz able to do it. Dey always got in de biggest kind of hurry. I noticed too I didn't feel bad like I had been feelin'. I had been keepin' de swimmin' in de haid and all kind of bad feelins, but dis old lady saved my life. I told two or three folks 'bout de remedy and all of 'em say it had done 'em good, too."

Uncle Ned, the Conjureman[6]

"As I told you before, my daddy come from Virginny. He wuz brought ter McDonough as a slave boy. Well as the speculator drove along south, he learned who the different slaves wuz. When daddy got here he wuz told by the master to live with old Uncle Ned 'cause he wuz the only bachelor on the plantation. The master said to old Ned, 'Well Ned, I have bought me a fine young plow boy. I want him to stay with you and you treat him right.' Every night Uncle Ned would make a pallet on the floor for daddy and make him go to bed. When he got in, Uncle Ned would watch him out of the corner of his eye, but daddy would pretend he wuz asleep and watch old Uncle Ned to see what he wuz going ter do. After a while Uncle Ned would take a broom and sweep the fireplace clean, then he would get a basket and take out of it a whole lot of little bundles wrapped in white cloth. As he lay out a package he would say 'grass hoppers,' 'spiders,' 'scorpion,' 'snake heads,' etc., then he would take the tongs and turn 'em around before the blaze so that they would parch. Night after night he would do this same thing until they parched enough, then he would beat all of it together and make a powder; then put it up in little bags. My daddy wuz afraid to ask old Uncle Ned what he did with those bags, but heard he conjured folks with 'em. In fact he did conjure a gal 'causd she wouldn't pay him no 'tention. This gal wuz very young and preferred talking to the younger men, but Uncle Ned always tried ter hang around her and help her, but she would always tell him to go do his own work 'cause she could do hers. One day he said to her 'All right, I'll see you later; you won't notice me now but you'll wish you had.' When the dinner came and they left the fields, they left their hoes standing so they would know just where ter start when they got back. When the gal went back ter the field the minute she touched that hoe she fell dead. Some folks say they saw Uncle Ned dressing that hoe with conjure.

The Conjured Peach Tree[7]

"My sister Lizzie she did get fixed, honey, and it took a old conjurer ter get the spell out of her. It wuz like this: Sister Lizzie had a pretty peach tree and one limb spreaded out over the walk and just as soon as she would walk under this limb, she would stay sick all the time. The funny part 'bout it wuz that while she wuz at other folk's house she would feel all right, but the minute she passed under this limb, she would begin ter feel bad. One day she sent for a conjurer, and he looked under the house, and sho nuff, he found it stuck in the sill. It looked like a bundle of rags, red flannel all stuck up with needles and everything else. This old conjurer told her that the tree had been dressed for her and t'would be best for her ter cut it down. It was a pretty tree and she did hate to cut it down, but she did like he told her. Yes child, I don't know whither I've ever been conjured or not, but sometimes my head hurts and I wonder."

The Conjured Farmer

A man in Fannin County said he was bewitched by a woman in the community because his cow gave clabbered milk, his hogs had fits and the steer he was plowing had its hip thrown out of place. He cut the tips of the hogs' ears off and the ends of their tails and walked backwards to the house without speaking and placed them under a hearth rock. The hogs, cow and steer got well. He was asked how he knew that this particular woman was the cause of it. He said that one night he had been up with his sick wife, and the weather being hot, he had left the door open and gone back to sleep. He heard the door creak and looking up he saw the woman come in with a bridle. She saw him get up and ran. He said she planned to make a mule out of him and put the bridle on and ride him.

This man grew so afraid of this neighboring woman's influence that he sold his farm and moved to another county.

SOURCES

1. Informant: Mrs. Julia Rush, ex-slave. Atlanta. Field Worker: Edwin Driskell. 1937.
2. Informant: Carrie Fryer. Augusta. Field Worker: Maude Barragan.
3. Augusta. Field Worker: Maude Barragan.
4. Informant: Mildred Price, ex-slave. Augusta. Field Worker: Louise Oliphant.
5. Informant: Frances Wright. Augusta. Field Worker: Louise Oliphant.
6. Informant: Celestine Avery, ex-slave. Atlanta. Field Worker: Lillian Milner.

spit on it, place it in the same spot from which you took it. This will stop the pain.

For a sprained ankle or wrist, dig a hole in the ground until you reach the red dirt. Then bury the sprained part in the hole for three or more hours.

Apply a poultice made with a mixture of red clay and vinegar.

To cure a crick in the neck, rub the sufferer's neck against a tree where a hog has rubbed itself.

5. Stomach Ache

To cure stomach ache drink tea made of pennyroyal or scalamus root, or wild mint, or snake root, or from the lining of a chicken's gizzard.

Tea made with the root of sumac when given with browned corn meal seasoned with pepper and salt cures colitis.

Gather the stones under the drip-off of the porch. Boil, and drink the water when cold.

6. Toothache

Hold whiskey in the mouth to kill the pain.

Take two lighter (pine) splinters and sharpen the ends of both. Dig in where the tooth hurts until there is blood on the end of both splinters. Take a knife and the two splinters and go into the woods where there are dogwood trees. On the north side of a dogwood tree place the splinters in a hole and cover them. By the time you get back home the toothache will be gone.

Shoot a bullet into some fresh meat to cure toothache.

A "tooth doctor" can conjure toothache by writing a word on a piece of paper, folding it many times, then tying a string around it and hanging it around his neck while saying some mysterious words.

ATHLETE'S FOOT

For athlete's foot or tender and blistered feet, soak the feet in warm salt water, and apply kerosene to the soles.

BLEEDING

Soot applied to wounds will stop bleeding.

Take nine joints of mulberry roots or nine buttons and string and tie them around your neck, or tie around the littlest finger a string made from raw cotton to stop bleeding.

Drop scissors down your back to cure nose bleeding.

Put a spoon or a bunch of keys down the back to stop nose bleed.

An axe beneath a bed will cut off hemorrhage.

Cooling remedies applied to a knife or to an axe that has made a bad cut, instead of to the wound itself, heals the cut.

Spider webs are applied to the cut to staunch the flow of blood, for that is what house spiders were created for, and it is bad luck to destroy them or their webs.

To stop severe flow of blood: Say aloud or read Ezekiel 16:6: "And when I passed by thee and saw thee polluted in thine own blood, I said unto thee when thou wast in thy blood, Live; yes, I said unto thee thou wast in thy blood, Live."

Salt tied in the tail of the shirt of the sufferer will stop uterine hemorrhages.

Put a piece of newspaper between your upper lip and gum and it will cure nose bleeding.

Brown paper soaked in vinegar placed on the palate in the mouth will stop nose bleeding when other crude remedies fail.

BOILS AND RISIN'S

Boils or risin's can be cured by applying a poultice of Irish potato scrapings, house leak root, cow dung, alder bark tea, or bread and milk.

BRUISES

Bind bruise with a fresh, salted chicken gizzard; if no chicken gizzard is available, apply a raw Irish potato.

Bind a bruised or sprained limb in a clay and vinegar poultice.

BURNS

If you get a severe burn get some one versed in the magic to talk the fire out of the burn.

Make a salve by boiling sweet gum bark, lard and a handful of Balm of Gilead buds.

Place the burned part of the body in cold water.

Apply a poultice of butter, the white of an egg, or soda and sewing machine oil.

Put "drundle" of kindlin' in the fire, and hold the burn near it.

CHILLS AND FEVER

To cure chills and fever, pull down the cover as if going to bed, then get under the bed. The chills and fever, being fooled, will not follow you.

Boil boneset stems in water to a strong tea and give to fever patient. Drink the tea very hot, keep patient covered up thoroughly and sweat out the fever.

If you are having three-day chills and fever, crawl down the stairs headforemost just before the time for the rigor to set in.

Hang onions in the house and if anyone in the room has a temperature, the fever will go to the onions.

Blue stone in tea is a good remedy for the fever.

Wrap the body in cold, bruised, wet collard leaves. Bind them to the wrist and forehead, too, for fever.

Bruise peach tree leaves, dip in salty vinegar and apply to body.

Make a tea of dog fennel, drink it warm and bathe in it hot.

COLIC

Drink blacksnake root tea or charred corn dust tea.

Drink asafetida in whiskey.

A string with seven knots in it is tied about one's stomach to avoid colic.

Pour boiling water over catnip and steep. Add enough sugar to make palatable for baby colic.

Steep soot in hot water and give to a baby every half hour.

CORNS

To rid yourself of a corn, grease it with a mixture of castor oil and kerosene and then soak in warm water.

Place a fat salt pork scrap on a corn. Do this every night for at least a week.

CRAMPS

A string with seven knots tied around the waist will keep cramps away.

Wear a raw cotton string tied in nine knots around your waist to cure cramps.

Turn both shoes bottom-side up with soles touching as in standing with feet together.

Wear an eel skin around the leg. This serves as a sure preventive of cramp in the leg.

A narrow strap of leather worn on the wrist prevents cramps.

Remove the left shoe first at night. This will prevent cramps.

Wear a copper band around the ankle to cure cramps.

DEBUGGING

To kill redbugs (chiggars), bathe with water and lye soap, then smear body with soft butter.

To kill lice and nits, smear hair and head with soft butter mixed with tobacco tea.

Make a ring around your ankles with kerosene to keep red bugs from getting on you.

DIABETES

Open the black spot, and let the puss pour out. Make a poultice with lard and meal one day, and scraped Irish potato (raw) the next. Bathe in hot epsom salts when you change the poultice.

DOG BITE

Should you receive a dog bite, take some of the hair from the dog's belly and bind it into the wound.

Bind a piece of fat salt pork to the wound.

A mad stone is a hard porous stone secured from the liver of a deer, and which can frequently be used successfully in the cure of the bite of a snake or of a rabid dog.

DYSENTERY

Boil blackberry root in water, make strong tea, and drink.

Eat broiled fat bacon without bread.

Take nine dog-fennel blooms and put in water. It will cure vomiting as well as dysentery.

Drink yellow jasmine root tea, watermelon seed tea, burned cornbread tea, blackberry root tea, crow foot tea, or wild sage tea.

Take roots from scurvy grass or ricket weed, boil and make a tea. Drink a cupful at night and in the morning.

Smear the white of an egg to the abdomen. Also, feed the white of an egg to a child to cure dysentery.

EYE PROBLEMS

Snow water and rain drippings from off the black walnut tree cure sore eyes.

To cure sore eyes, wash them in a mule trough.

Place potato peelings over an inflammed eye to draw out the soreness.

Frozen urine, melted and mixed with snow-water, will cure blindness.

To cure a stye rub it with a cat's tail.

To cure a stye, go to the forks of a road, stand directly in the center of the forks saying, "Stye, stye, leave my eye and catch the first one who comes by."

Rub a gold ring on the stye and it will vanish.

A stye may be cured by looking at a friend who tells you the stye will disappear. You must believe the person.

Stand on a corner when you have a stye and say this verse, "Stye, stye, leave my eye and catch the first one that passes by."

FROSTBITE

To cure frostbite apply a boiled turnip poultice.

GOITER

Look at the new moon and rub the goiter while saying, "What I see increases, what I see increases, what I see increases," and "What I feel decreases, what I feel decreases, what I feel decreases." The goiter goes away.

Wear a black velvet ribbon around your neck to get rid of a goiter.

Wear amber beads around the neck to cure goiter.

HEMORRHOIDS

Black snuff, alum, a piece of camphor, and red vaseline mixed together is a sure cure for "piles."

A buckeye carried will prevent hemorrhoids.

HICCOUGHS

Hiccoughs will disappear if you drink nine sips of water while holding your breath.

If a person has hiccoughs, give him a sudden scare or a big surprise. This will suddenly take his mind off himself and his hiccoughs will stop.

To stop hiccoughs, cross two straws on the top of your head.

Hold your breath and count to ten and the hiccoughs will be gone.

Lick the back of your hand and swallow nine times without stopping to cure hiccoughs.

HIVES

Place a child with hives in a chimney and shake him. If that fails get a man who has never seen his own father to blow in the child's face.

Drink catnip tea or sheep dung tea to cure hives.

INFLAMMATION

Make a strong tea of red oak bark and mix in meal and cook to a mush. Make a poultice by spreading on a cloth while hot and place it on a wound for drawing out inflammation. Peach tree leaves or gourd guts and molasses prepared in the same manner may be used also.

Scrape raw beet, make a poultice, and put on wound or sore to draw out inflammation and cool fever.

Place a raw piece of steak on sore place to draw inflammation.

Three small doses of morphine will kill bone-felon.

Drink silver grass tea.

Take six moth balls, one cup of table salt and one quart of gasoline. Mix together. Pat it on the swelling.

Make an incision in the back of a live frog in such a manner as not to produce instant death, and bind to the affected finger to cure bone-felon.

INSECT BITES AND STINGS

Tobacco poultices are good for insect bites and to check ringworm.

To immunize man or beast from poisonous insect bites, smear body or exposed parts with toad oil.

Tobacco oil applied to wasp or bee stings will allay the pain.

Peach seeds, powdered to a pulp and mixed with flour dough and honey, make a good poultice for bee stings, mosquito and spider bites.

Put mud on the part stung by a bee or a hornet.

Wash a sting with turpentine.

INGROWN TOE NAIL

Cut the nail in the moonlight under water.

KIDNEY TROUBLE

Old field pine will cure kidney trouble.

Eating of raisins cures kidney ailments.

For Bright's disease and other kidney troubles, consume large quantities of onions, raw or cooked in any style desired.

MALARIA

Dogwood and cherry bark tea is given for curing fevers caused by malaria. To make it more effective add red oak bark.

For malaria douse the body with quince-seed tea.

MEASLES

To force measles to break out, drink tea made of water and the boiled dung of sheep.

To avoid measles, swallow three buckshot each day until nine have been taken.

Catnip tea is a panacea for measles.

Put lemons by the bed and they will break out measles on people that have difficulty breaking out. The lemons will break out too.

Wear sulphur in your shoes to prevent seven years' itch, measles and other skin diseases.

MENINGITIS

Beat charcoal to a fine dust, add turpentine, kerosene, lard and cornmeal and then make a plaster. Spread it thickly all over the back and then sew on a tight jacket to make it secure.

MENSTRUATION

For monthly pains make a hot tea of squaw weed or horse-mint and drink before you go to bed. Squaw weed grows wild and has yellow blossoms.

Tea made from parched egg shells or green coffee is good for preventing excessive bleeding, and it keeps off the ills of menopause.

MUMPS

To cure mumps break the boiled jaw bone of a hog, take out the marrow and make a poultice of it and apply to victim's jaws and throat. Hog jowl rubbed on the jaws also helps cure mumps.

Put a colored silk band or a black string around neck.

NIGHT SWEATS

If a person has night sweats, put a pan of cold water under his bed without his knowledge. He will not have another sweat.

OBESITY

For obesity, eat lean meat, rye bread, and leafy vegetables.

POISON OAK

Make a tincture by boiling yellow dock root ten minutes in pure apple vinegar. Sponge with it.

Wash the infected parts with a salt water mixture.

PREVENTING CONTAGIOUS DISEASES

A nutmeg tied about the neck will ward off diseases.

A child will be spared contagious diseases if a boiled egg in a cloth bag is suspended above its bed.

The wearing of onions or camphor gum, or sulphur or asafetida, or chinchona bark, or poke berry roots, myrrh, or sassafras in a bag about the neck shields a child from contagious diseases.

Mince a rabbit and a stalk of celery and eat the mixture. It will give you internal strength sufficient to accelerate the secretions of the glands of digestion. It is a preventive of most diseases.

A bright copper wire twisted around the leg or wrist is said to be a sure preventive for most diseases. The cooper is to be worn always, whether the flesh underneath festers or not. The preventive will not work should the cooper ever be removed.

A silver dime with a hole in it strung and fastened around the leg is also a charm against all diseases.

If you wear a red onion around your waist it will keep you from contracting contagious diseases.

The left hind leg of a graveyard rabbit is general protection against all manner of evil and disease.

Asafetida tied around the neck prevents smallpox.

Touching an animal on the part of the body which corresponds to that of the stricken sufferer will cause the transference of the pain to the animal.

RESPIRATORY AILMENTS

Boil down the bark of the root of a wild plum tree and drink in place of water or milk for three days to cure asthma.

Drink fodder tea for asthma.

Roast a big yellow onion before the fire until tender and juicy, mash well and sprinkle with sugar for bronchial cough.

Fat pine splinters boiled down in water, mixed with whiskey and rock candy are good for bronchial cough.

Soak green pine needles (bruised) in water and drink all through the day in place of water for colds and bronchitis.

Boil fat lightwood splinters, strain the water, thicken with honey, boil to syrup; when cool, add paragoric (a tablespoonful to a half pint of water). Take three or four times a day for cough.

Chew sweet gum and elbow root. Boil down sweet gum and mullein, add honey and boil to a syrup and use for bronchial cough.

Put turpentine on sugar and take it for a cough.

Make a strong tea of rabbit tobacco or the bud of a pine sapling and fat pine splinters or a pulverized hog's hoof. Drink warm.

Put kerosene, turpentine, and tallow on a flannel cloth and heat it and put it on your chest for deep chest colds and coughs.

The remedies for common cold are many. Wrap wool yarn around ankles or wrists and leave it until it comes off of its own accord when the cold is well.

Rub hog foot oil on the soles of the feet for severe summer and winter colds. Repeat often.

Pour boiling water over Samson snake root, or red roots, or dog fennel and then drink.

Take hot mustard foot-bath for colds, croup, and grippe.

Gargle with a mixture of salt, vinegar, and water.

Wear amber beads to avoid croup.

Melted hog lard with a little sugar and turpentine added, when taken internally or when applied externally as a poultice, is good for croup.

For pulmonary troubles eat fat salt pork and drink pine tar tea flavored with honey and whiskey.

A toad tied with a string to a bed post in which a person is suffering from whooping cough will expedite the cure.

If you want to cure whooping cough you may make tea out of rabbit tobacco.

Drink out of a horse or mule trough.

Drink either mare's milk or toad frog soup for whooping cough.

Put a baby in a hopper and grind the corn out from under it, and the baby will not have whooping cough.

Whooping cough can be prevented by swallowing three live minnows.

RHEUMATISM

The pain and crippling effects of rheumatism have occasioned the wearing of many charms against this disease: a dime with a hole in it, a coil of copper, a steel ring, an eel skin around the wrist, or a dried rattlesnake skin about the affected part. A nutmeg worn around the neck so that it touches the breastbone or solar plexus, the great nerve center, is another cure. Or bore a hole in the nutmeg; the aromatic oil exuding therefrom will be absorbed by the body and soothe the nerves afflicted.

Take fresh tender leaves of polk, parboil, and season as you do turnip greens, and eat in the spring of the year for a blood tonic and rheumatism.

Drink elderberry tea or blackberry root tea and rub the afflicted area with rattlesnake oil.

Carry a buckeye in the pocket to cure rheumatism or a rabbit bone in the pocket for the same cure.

Make a stew of earthworms and water and rub the concoction on the affected parts.

A salve of stolen butter will cure rheumatism.

Steal an Irish potato and carry in the pocket to cure rheumatism.

SHINGLES

Blood of a black cat or a black hen rubbed on the affected parts of the body will cure shingles.

Catch a black hen and pull off her head. Hold the neck so that the blood streams over the shingles. Have a cloth around the body to catch the blood. When all the blood has been used pull up this cloth and use it as a poultice. Leave it there as long as it will stick. Don't pull it or move it at all, and the shingles will have disappeared when it falls off.

SNAKE BITE

An open bottle of turpentine held over a snake bite will draw out the poison into the turpentine.

If a person is bitten on the leg or arm, dig a hole and bury the limb in the earth for from twelve to twenty-four hours.

For rattlesnake bite, drink large quantities of cockleburr tea.

For rattlesnake bite, cut open a frog and place the cut over the bite before the frog is dead. As the frog dies, it will draw the poison from the wound into its own body.

Cut through the bite; then put the cut inside a freshly-killed chicken (don't bother to pick the feathers). Leave the wound there till the chicken is cold. The chicken will turn black. You must not use the chicken for anything else.

To cure a snake bite, split a toad in half with a very sharp knife or razor, and apply alternately first one half of the toad and then the other half to the wound.

Drink a lot of whiskey and you will not feel the pain.

Suck the poison from the wound and then spit it out.

SORE MOUTH, SORE THROAT, AND TONSILITIS

Common salt and cooking soda, diluted in warm water, makes an effective gargle for tonsilitis and sore throat. One can also gargle with vinegar and black pepper.

To cure sore mouth among children, give them seven sips of water from the heel of a shoe that has been worn by one who was born after their father died.

Sore mouth will be cured by holding honey in it.

A piece of flannel or stocking tied loosely around the neck will cure sore throat.

Urine mixed with ashes and worn as a poultice around the neck will cure a sore throat.

Horehound tea is good for sore throat.

To relieve sore throat or coughing, lift a few locks of hair in the crown of the head.

SPLINTERS

Fat salt pork will draw out splinters.

SUNSTROKE

To avoid sun stroke wear moistened willow or beech leaves inside the hat.

If your eyes burn and your head aches from too much glare, bind jimson weed leaves or elderberry leaves to the head.

TONICS FOR BLOOD

Soak roots of burdock in whiskey and take as blood tonic after measles.

For sluggish blood, take an occasional pinch of sulphur.

To purify the blood, drink poplar bark tea or cherry bark tea, or dogwood bark tea or swamp elder bark tea.

Bitters made of dogwood, poplar, and wild cherry bark make a good spring tonic.

Boil down wild cherry bark, sweet gum and mullein to a concentrated tea, mix with honey and make syrup. Use for a general tonic.

TUBERCULOSIS

Half-fill a bottle with table salt, then fill it with good whiskey. Drink it all through the day.

Rural Folk Were Their Own Doctors

TYPHOID

A string of red onions tied around the bed of a typhoid victim will shrivel as it absorbs the fever.

WARTS

Some people are reputed to have power to cure warts by rubbing them with their fingers and mumbling strange words over them.

To cure warts, bathe them with water caught in a rotten stump. The application should be repeated three times.

Prick a wart until it bleeds. Take a stone, put a drop of blood on it, wrap it in a paper and put it in the middle of a road. The person who picks up the package will get the warts and thereby relieve the sufferer.

Rub the wart on a dead body. When the corpse begins to decay the wart will go away.

Tie a thread around the middle of a wart and it will soon disappear.

Rub a wart with an apple, then tie the apple by a string to your bedroom door. When the apple rots off the string, the wart will drop off.

To remove a wart, pare until it bleeds and rub with the juice of red oak bark, or apply wood ashes.

Rub a wart with buckshot, then drop the buckshot into a toad's mouth.

Stick a brass pin into a wart; apply heat to the head of the pin; then withdraw and bury it in a pile of ashes.

Seed beans or peas which have warts on their roots will cause warts on the body to disappear as soon as they sprout.

Find a stump (gum stump preferred) with water in it. Immerse wart in the stump water and repeat "go away wart" three times. Then walk away from the stump without looking back and the wart will soon disappear.

Pick the seed out of a wart; burn it, and the wart will dry up.

Pick a wart until it bleeds; smear the blood on a piece of bread or a grain of corn, and feed to a chicken.

Dip warts into mud where hogs wallow, or rub mud on a tree.

Steal a dish cloth and rub on the wart to take it off.

Sell your wart to a friend for a penny. Lose the penny and you will also lose the wart.

Scratch a tic-tac-toe cross on thumb nail and recite a secret Bible verse to remove wart.

Scratch a wart until it bleeds, steal a greasy dish rag, wipe the blood off with the greasy rag and throw the rag away; the wart will disappear.

Rub a black-eyed pea on a wart, put it in a sack and blow up the sack. Tie it with a string as if full of something, throw it out on the street or highway, and if someone picks it up the wart will disappear.

Make a cross on the wart with a needle or pin and stick it in the sufferer's collar where it will fall out. When it falls off the wart will disappear; if anyone picks it up the wart will be transferred to him.

Make as many holes in a piece of paper as there are warts to take off, and drop it at a crossroads. Go away without looking back. But don't let any of your friends pick up the paper, for whoever does will get all the warts.

WORMS

Eat horehound candy, raw garlic without salt, or chinaberries.

Make a syrup from the bark of Jerusalem oak and drink it.

Drink pumpkin seed tea to dislodge worms in children.

SOURCES

1. This verse was quoted by Informant: Mrs. Melvine Douglas, ex-slave. Columbus. Field Worker: M. H. Dauphin. Jan., 1937.
2. A few examples of folk medicine appear in almost every report in the collection. The following are the identifiable important sources.
   Informant: Emma Coker, Negro. Augusta. Field Worker: Maude Barragan. May, 1937.
   Informant: Carrie Nancy Fryer, Negro. Augusta. Field Worker: Maude Barragan. Nov., 1937.
   Informant: Julia Henderson, Negro. Augusta. Field Worker: Maude Barragan. Jan., 1937.
   Informant: Julia Rush, Negro. Atlanta. Field Worker: Edwin Driskell. No date.
   Informant: Mattie Singleton, Negro. Atlanta. Field Worker: W. W. Linton. No date.
   Informant: Sallie Carter White, Negro. Rome. Field Worker: Mary Lawton. No date.

CHAPTER V

S U P E R S T I T I O N S

Of all the forms of folklore collected in this volume, none has proved more persistent than the superstitions. Many of these beliefs remain as common as they were a century ago. A neighbor who professes no belief in the supernatural spilled salt at a recent dinner party and immediately threw some of the spilled grains over his left shoulder to ward off bad luck. A professor with whom we occasionally play poker refuses to hand cards to anyone at the table because he insists, "You're handing out your good luck." A fellow gardener warned against planting a willow tree because "It will weep for its owner's death." Last year at a family reunion an aunt refused to seat thirteen at a table. Even in highly sophisticated society superstitions persist.

Superstitions are among the humblest forms of folk literature, but for that very reason they often reveal more intensely than other forms the society which produced and nourished them. For example, in a region such as Georgia which has much traditional rural poverty one would expect to find many superstitions concerning wealth. The state abounds with superstitions such as these: a dream of a white horse means the dreamer will find money; if you wish for wealth while looking over your left shoulder at a new moon, you receive it; it is a sign that you will be rich if a blue bird flies into your house or if a spider crawls upon you.

From the days when travel in Georgia was difficult and a long trip demanded much preparation, one finds numerous folk beliefs surrounding the journey. You dared not leave on a Friday or bad luck would follow. You carried a rabbit foot with you for good luck, and you stuffed your ears with cotton to keep from hearing or absorbing any evil on the road.

The rural man often saw signs in the natural events of his life, and if some superstition came true once it was enough for a lifetime belief. If a dove flew over the house, you would receive a sad message. If you bit your tongue, you had recently told a lie. If you found sand in your shoe, you would return to the very spot where it came from whether you wanted to or not. If a firefly got into your house, a stranger was coming.

Historically both rural and urban society in Georgia have abounded in superstitions, and then, as now, the superstitious man knew his beliefs were irrational. However, a man's actions seldom depend upon what he considers rational. A Georgia pawnbroker of a generation ago would make a heavy sacrifice to sell to the first customer on a Monday morning, believing that it meant prosperity for the entire week. The first customer got no less of a bargain because he did not believe that superstition. Fate was tempted by one who walked under a ladder or whose path was crossed by a black cat. Belief, whether rational or not, is often more important in human affairs than facts. The superstitions collected here concern dreaming, wishing, good luck, bad luck, buildings, beds, journeys, and signs.

D R E A M S[1]

To dream of the dead means it will rain.

To dream of seeing a lot of uncooked fresh meat means death of someone well known.

To dream of seeing a train moving means you will soon take a trip.

To dream of seeing fruit out of season foretells trouble out of reason.

To dream of counting paper money means good luck.

To dream of clear water means good luck; muddy water, bad luck.

To dream of a rabbit signifies physical weakness.

To dream of gathering roses means you will win whom you wish.

To dream of caskets is a sign of death. You may expect to hear of as many deaths as there are caskets in the dream.

To dream of blood is a sign of trouble.

To dream of fish is a sign of motherhood.

To dream of eggs is a sign of trouble unless the eggs are broken. If the eggs are broken, your trouble is ended.

To dream of snakes is a sign of enemies. If you kill the snakes, you have conquered your enemies.

To dream of fire is a sign of danger.

To dream of a funeral is a sign of a wedding.

To dream of a wedding is a sign of a funeral.

To dream of silver money is a sign of bad luck; of bills, good luck.

To dream of yellow flowers means someone is jealous of you. Beware!

To dream of a white horse is good luck.

To dream of black horses, death comes near your people.

To dream of finding money is a sign that some form of good luck will visit the dreamer.

To dream of muddy waters or of crossing a swollen stream portends a death in the family of the dreamer.

To dream of flying is a sign of approaching evil.

To dream of hell is a warning to change your mode of life. To dream of heaven is a sign that you are living right.

To dream of a great deal of meat is an indication of death.

To dream of a naked woman means a man's death and to dream of a naked man means a woman's death.

Take warning if you dream of rushing to catch a train, for it means you are overworked or are pushing yourself too hard.

To dream of wild animals foretells trouble with your debts.

To dream of falling, everything will be all right if you don't land, but if you hit bottom, you will die.

To dream of holding a new-born baby, some new interest is coming into your life.

The dream of white horses is a forecast that new power and strength is coming to you.

Trouble will drown your joy if you dream of black, muddy waters; to dream of running black water means trouble will come and pass away.

To dream of a cat, you are being deceived.

To dream of crying is a sign of trouble.

To dream of dancing is a sign of happiness.

Any dream you tell before breakfast will come true.

When you dream while under a new quilt, your dream will come true.

Whatever you dream the first night you sleep in a new house will come true.

WISHING[2]

When you see the first star in the evening, repeat:

Star light, star bright,
First star I've seen tonight;
I wish I may, I wish I might,
Have the wish I wish tonight.

Then make a wish and it will come true.

If you see a load of unbaled hay, repeat:

Load of hay, load of hay,
Give me the wish I wish today.

Throw a kiss at it, and do not look at it again; you will then get your wish.

When a white horse appears, lick your thumb, press it in the palm of your other hand. Stamp the place with your fist and say:

Cross-cross,
White hoss,
Money for the week's done.

And you will get your wish.

Make a wish upon seeing a white mule. It will come true if you do not look back.

If you find a horseshoe spit on it, make a wish, and throw it over your left shoulder. If you can't see it when you look back your wish will come true.

If two people say the same thing at the same time they must lock the little fingers on their right hands and make a wish. Then one says "Shakespeare," the other "Lowell," one "needles," the other "pins." Make a wish. Don't tell, and it will come true.

If you find a loose eyelash, hold it between the thumb and forefinger and make a wish. Then guess to which it will stick. If you guess correctly your wish will come true.

Find a pin, stick it in your left shoulder, and make a wish. If it falls out before the day is over, your wish will not come true.

If you see a white horse, clap your palms together twice and make a wish.

Make a wish while watching a turkey buzzard "sailing." If the wish is fully expressed before he flaps his wings, the wish will come true.

When you are served a piece of pie, cut the point off and save it for the last bite; make a wish and it will come true.

If you find half a shoe, turn it one-half way around without moving it off the ground and any wish you make will come true.

When you see a red bird, blow a kiss to the bird and make a wish. The wish will come true.

Making a wish while looking over your shoulder at the new moon, clear of any brush or trees, will insure the fulfillment of the wish.

It is good luck to look into a well on the first day of May and make a wish.

If someone's shoe comes untied and the one who ties it makes a wish, the wish will come true.

When a person puts a ring on another person's finger he makes a wish and tells the other person when to remove the ring so that the wish will come true. If the ring is removed before the date set, the wish will not come true.

When you throw a stone into a pond or lake, make a wish before the first circle disappears and it will come true.

If a person goes into a strange church and makes a wish, he will get it before the year is out.

Make up a rhyme when you hear a beautiful strain of music and your dearest wish will be granted.

If you stand on a stone that cannot be moved and make a wish, you will get the wish.

Go into a graveyard and dip your hands into a vessel of clear water, and any wish you make then will come true.

When you find a stone broken in halves, place the two parts together, throw them over the right shoulder and wish.

If you pull wish bones, the one who gets the junction of the bone does not get his wish.

If a person will make a wish, then cut an apple in halves without cutting a seed, it is a sign the wish will be fulfilled.

Stamp an eyelash down on the back of your hand, make a wish and blow; if you blow it off, you will have your wish.

If a wild animal crosses the road in front of you, make a wish and it will be granted.

If two people say the same thing, they both must join little fingers and make a wish. Then the following dialogue takes place:

> "Needles"—"Pins"
> "Sweetheart"—"Friends"
> "What goes up the chimney?"—"Smoke."
> "What goes down the chimney?"—"Santa Claus."

Then both make a wish and each will come true.

If you wish when you enter a covered bridge and hold your breath all the way, you get your wish.

If all the candles on your birthday cake go out at a breath, your wish will come true.

GOOD LUCK

(Charms[3], Insuring Luck[4], Signs of Good Luck[5])

It is good luck
    to carry the right front foot of a mole;
    to find a coin and keep it;
    to wear a dime fastened around your ankle;
    to meet a preacher at a road crossing;
    to drop a fork on the breakfast table on Sunday
      morning;
    to meet a person with a bundle.

Buckeyes and nutmegs carried in the pocket bring good luck.

To offer a prayer while touching dogwood berries carries one's petition straight to the ears of the Savior, for was not Christ's cross made of dogwood? Ever since His Crucifixion the beautiful white flowers have had a crimp in each petal symbolic of the scars made by the nails through the hands of Jesus.

Shoe strings made of corn shucks worn in work shoes bring good luck.

A rabbit's foot should be carried in the right-hand pocket to bring the best luck; it is also deemed wise to pour whiskey on your rabbit's foot once in a while to keep it in good working order. It is better if the rabbit was killed in a graveyard on a night in the dark of the moon.

A ball of human hair, carried in a bag made from a scrap of a woman's discarded underwear, will bring a man good luck.

Finding an old horseshoe in the road brings good luck if you hang it prongs-up over your door. An especially effective horseshoe is one worn thin and rusty and having lots of nails left in it.

You can change your luck by throwing a teaspoon full of sulphur into a fire at exactly noon.

If a cook will carry in her apron pocket the dry skin that a snake has shed and rub her hands on it at intervals, she will never break any dishes.

Throw a pocket full of money into the front door on New Year's Day to insure good luck all year. The more money it contains the better will be your luck.

Hog jowls and peas on New Year's Day bring prosperity throughout the year.

To insure luck stick a pin in the first tree you come near.

If salt is spilled, quickly throw some over the left shoulder to ward off evil; also, full salt cellars at New Year's bring prosperity.

It is good luck to wear one sock of one color and one of another.

If unlucky while playing cards, walk around the table three times to change your luck.

Spit on dice before throwing them.

Spitting in his glove brings good luck to a baseball player.

Kill the first snake you see in spring.

When playing bridge sit on a handerchief.

If you start somewhere and forget something, you must make a cross mark and spit on it to insure good luck.

Don't sweep dirt away from your door; if you do, you will sweep all your luck away.

Every time you see a white horse, stamp the palm of the left hand by moistening the forefinger of the right hand and touching it to the palm of the left hand, then stamp with the fist of right hand.

Plant a holly tree. If it lives, good luck; if it dies, death comes to someone in the family.

It is good luck if you wear a garment wrong side out provided someone not kin to you turns it right for you; otherwise, it is better to wear the garment wrong side out to the end of the day.
It is a sign of good luck if your knife sticks up when you drop it.
A sign of good luck is to go along the streets on a Monday morning and find buttons.

It is said to be lucky for two persons to run into each other accidentally.

When a red bird flies in front of you something unexpectedly good will happen.

It is considered to be a sign of unfailing good luck to discover the new moon on the first night of its appearance, provided no tree limbs or other item obstructs the view.

If you are going up hill and see a new moon clearly, your luck will rise.

For a squirrel to run across the road in front of you is a sign of good luck.

For a butterfly to come into the house means good luck.

A man visitor on New Year's Day means good luck, but a woman visitor is bad luck.

A cricket in the house is a sign of good luck.

If a cat takes up with you it means good luck, unless the cat is black.

If a spider web brushes across one's face as he walks, it is a good luck sign.

To stub your right foot is good luck, but to stub your left foot is bad luck. To prevent the bad luck you must turn around three times.

See a white horse and look for a red-headed girl for good luck.

> *See a pin and let it lie,*
> *You'll need a pin before you die;*
> *See a pin and pick it up,*
> *All the day you'll have good luck.*

Objects made by blind people will bring luck to the possessors.

You must knock on wood after telling about good luck.

SUPERSTITIONS[6]

Signs of Bad Luck

Taking the last biscuit on the plate.

Sweeping the floor after sunset.

Hearing a hen crow before dawn.

Killing a cat.

Sewing on Sunday.

A rooster crowing on your front porch.

A collard plant going to seed.

Cutting paper on Sunday.

Turning a door knob completely around.

A raven or owl flying into your house.

Singing in bed.

Changing your name.

Meeting a coffin.

Starting something on Friday and not finishing it.

Stepping over anyone.

Turning a chair 'round and 'round on one leg.

Taking a ball bat out of someone's hand without first letting it touch the ground.

Brushing the hair after dark.

Burning your hair or letters.

Burning sassafras wood.

For a lightning bug or bird to fly into the house.

Carrying ashes out of the house at any time between Christmas and New Years.

Meeting a dog at night.

Meeting a tramp.

Toting a hoe or axe through the house on your shoulder, unless you take it back through the same door.

Showing a baby its reflection in a mirror.

Turning back after you start on a journey. To kill the jinx make a cross mark and spit on it.

Going with visitors to a stream and turning back without first crossing the stream.

Having a homeless black cat run across the road in front of you or take up at your house.

Seeing such a cat after dark, or keeping one.

Stepping over a broom or a fishing pole.

Finding a pin with the head toward you.

Fishing on Sunday.

Dreaming of an automobile.

Hearing roosters crowing after they have gone to roost.

Trimming the finger nails on Sunday or biting them off at any time.

Finding a button and keeping it a week.

Killing a dog or turtle dove.

Raising an umbrella in the house.

Courting with dust on your shoes.

Passing the salt directly to anyone at the table brings bad luck.

Setting in motion a rocking chair in which no one is sitting.

Scratching with the thumb-nail.

Leaving a room through one door and coming back through another.

Meeting a gray mule and a read headed woman the same day.

Owning guinea pigs.

Wearing an opal unless it is your birthstone.

Taking out ashes after sundown.

Letting the moon shine on fresh meat.

Giving or lending anything that has a sharp point such as a needle, a pin or scissors.

Saying good-bye over a stile.

Walking under a ladder.

Breaking a dish at a party.

Keeping in the house the feathers of a peacock.

Crossing over a bedmate when arising in the morning.

Turning over a chair.

Throwing trash out of doors after dark.

Lighting three cigarettes with one match.

Lending salt or red pepper.

Burning three lights in a room.

You will cry all day if your right eye itches.

Never give away something that was given you.

It is bad luck for one pedestrian to pass on the opposite side of a tree or part from his companion. Something is sure to come between the friends.

Shoes, when placed under a bed, should always have the toes point outward. Any deviation from this rule brings bad luck.

If you go away from any place and discover that you have left something, be sure to twist a hole in the ground with your heel an spit into it. That will ward off hard luck.

Never remove a wedding ring from somebody's finger.

Never walk in your shadow, unless you happen to pull a garment on wrong-side out; then stepping on your shadow breaks the evil spell cast by the act.

If a shoe string breaks, throw it away at once and get a new one. To mend a broken a shoe string is bad luck.

It is an invitation to hard luck to sweep a hallway after the early morning. If trash accumulates after the first sweeping it is safe to remove it with dust pan and brush.

You are passing out your own luck if you hand cards to anyone.

One who dies with her shoes on is doomed to have her soul wander.

For as many steps as one takes with one shoe on and one shoe off, he will have the same number of days of bad luck.

If a woman points out the new moon, you will have bad luck.

Do not cut down a tree in your yard, but dig it up to avoid bad luck.

You must step backward over a broom, for to step over it going forward is bad luck.

When a person leaves your house it is bad luck to stand at the door and watch that person until he or she is out of sight.

It is bad luck to move from a house and then at some later date move back into that same house.

It is unlucky to sew a button on a garment while wearing the garment, unless you hold a key in your mouth.

Put on the left shoe first to avoid bad luck.

It is unlucky to have a spinning wheel on board a ship; but lucky for a child to be born on board because then the ship will not sink.

If a rabbit runs across the road in front of you, to the left, it is a sign of bad luck.

If you go in a house and lay your hat on a bed it is bad luck.

If you go in the front door it is bad luck to go out the back.

To throw hair combings out of a window is bad luck; if birds use it for nest building you will have headaches.

BUILDINGS AND HOUSES[7]

Never begin building a house on Friday if you expect to get finished. If necessary, knock up a piece of frame on Thursday, no matter how late.

Do not burn wood of a tree that has been struck by lightning because your house will burn or be struck by lightning.

If rain does not descend on a new house until after the roof is on, the members of the house will be protected from trouble. If a strong wind blows away some loose part of a house while it is being build, woe will descend on the household.

Entering a new house for the first time on Sunday is excellent luck.

It is bad luck for the first person who enters a new house to go in by the back door. If this is done inadvertently, the person should immediately hop on the left foot backwards out of the house and at the bottom of the doorstep hop in a circle chanting:

> *I turn myself around,*
> *I turn myself around,*
> *I turn myself around,*
> *Back—Front,*
> *Luck*

Then go around to the front and enter the front door and the bad-luck spell is removed.

It is good luck to use in the construction of a house any lumber that has formerly been a part of a church.

No lumber cut from a tree that was "blasted by the hand of God," struck by lightning or felled by wind, should be used in house construction.

It is an old idea that the sleepers of a house should be made of oak; the walls, joists, rafters, and floors of pine; the shingles of cedar; and as many other kinds of wood as possible in its finishing.

A gambrel roof indicates, or was an invocation for, prosperity.

If the first flowers which are brought to a new house are roses, beware of enemies in the neighborhood and thorns that will prick beneath their smooth words. If lilies are brought, there will be a death in the family before the year is out. If simple garden posies are brought, there will be modest peace and contentment among the neighbors.

For a cat to take up at a new house is the best of luck, unless it is a black cat. If a black cat takes up, the only way to remove the bad luck is to pull three hairs out of the cat's tail, tie them together with a white thread and drop them in the first stream of water you cross.

J O U R N E Y S[8]

Never start a journey on Friday.

Never turn back for anything unless you draw a circle and step in it, or sit down and stay awhile.

If your foot itches, you are going to walk on new ground.

If, on starting on a journey, something to be taken along is forgotten and the traveler has to turn back, it is a bad omen.

Sew charms in the traveler's clothes as an antidote for any evil that might threaten him.

A traveler insures good luck if he brings home some of the food he had taken away with him.

To carry the left hind foot of a graveyard rabbit is a protection against the dangers of travel.

If a man's horse started off briskly, the traveler would have a pleasant journey, but if the horse started off sluggishly and without spirit, the trip would be an unpleasant one; if a dog howled, the man would be called back by a death in his family.

B E D S[9]

Unless your bed is pushed straight against the wall, you will have bad luck.

To sleep on a bed of corn shucks makes a person strong.

Beds made of hay bring peace and contentment to those who sleep on them.

Cotton mattresses are conducive to sound sleep.

Feather beds are conducive to fecundity.

Sleeping on a pine-straw mattress will cure consumption.

Sprigs of pennyroyal deposited under a bed will drive away fleas.

To sleep soundest and sweetest, place the head of a bed to the west—in the north corner of the room, thus facing the rising sun.

To prevent malaria, every bed should be three or more feet above the ground.

Tie a small bell to the bed-post; when evil spirits visit the sleeper the bell will frighten them away.

Heavy beds influence heavy sleep; light beds, light sleep.

If a rat runs across your bed, change the covers to prevent bad luck.

It is good luck for a cat to go to sleep on your bed.

GENERAL SIGNS[10]

If you hear a turtledove call in the morning you will move in that direction soon.

If a dove flies over a house a sad message is coming.

If you walk across the place where a horse has recently wallowed you will have a headache.

If you have a hole in your stocking you have a letter in the post office.

If you find a hairpin and hang it on a pine tree, you will surely have a letter by the next mail.

If you spill salt someone has told an untruthful story on you.

If you spill salt pick it up and throw it over your left shoulder with your right hand to avoid a quarrel with a friend.

If a spider gets on you it is a sign you will receive money.

If you burn bread there's going to be a fuss in the family.

To see all the stars clear at night is a good sign in business following any contract, agreement, or venture.

To see the stars in the morning after the sun is up indicates an increase in family or fortune.

If it rains on you through an open window, it is a sign you need a bath.

A person cleaning house should never sweep the lint out along with the other trash because in doing so he will be sweeping away his money.

Stub your toe and you will see your beau.

If foams and circles form around a cup of hot coffee, cream or tea, it is a sign you will get money.

If the left eye jumps the person is going to get very angry.

If, after you have taken a splinter from your hand, you run the splinter through your hair, the place will not hurt anymore.

If your right shoe comes unlaced, someone is saying good things about you; left shoe, bad things.

If a coal of fire falls from the fireplace a visitor is coming. If it is short and fat so too will be the visitor.

If a spark of fire pops on you, it is a sign that you will receive some money or a letter.

If you find sand in your shoes you will return to the spot where it came from, whether you wish to or not.

SIGNS OF CALLERS

If you place two biscuits on your plate, a hungry visitor is coming.

Dropping a dish rag means that a hungry visitor is coming.

A rooster crowing at your back door means a caller.

When you are washing dishes and drop a dish cloth, if it is in a knot a man is coming and if it falls loose, a woman is coming.

If a lightning bug gets into your house at night, a stranger is coming.

A butterfly entering the front door means guests are coming.

Tea leaves floating in a cup indicate that many visitors are coming.

Spilling of salt is the sign that someone hungry is coming to your home.

When the palm of your right hand itches, you will greet a stranger.

If you sneeze before you get out of bed, someone is coming. If you sneeze while eating, you must rinse out your mouth or there will be a death in the family.

If the tip of the nose itches somebody is coming by car or on horseback.

If a small child picks up a broom and tries to sweep, somebody is coming.

A hornet in the house is a sign that a stranger is coming.

A spider hanging on a web from the ceiling signifies that a stranger is coming.

When a spider builds a web in your house, you may expect a visitor the same color as the spider.

If you have company on Monday you will have it all the week.

To drop a knife, a woman is coming; a fork, a man is coming; a big spoon, a girl is coming; a teaspoon, the whole family is coming.

ITCHING SIGNS

A burning ear indicates that its owner is being talked about disparagingly.

When a person's right hand itches it is a sign that the person is soon to receive some money.

If one's foot itches, he will travel soon.

If one's fingers itch, he will grasp something pleasant or of value.

If your right eye itches you will cry. If your left eye itches you will be pleased.

If your right ear burns somebody is talking good about you; if your left ear burns somebody is talking meanly about you.

You will kiss a fool if your nose itches.

If the palm of your left hand itches you will receive money, provided you rub the palm on wood, close the hand, and put it in the pocket; if the palm of the right hand itches you will shake hands with a stranger.

If your foot itches, you are going to walk on strange land.

If a person's left eye itches it is a sign that he will soon cry about something. If the right eye itches it is a sign that he will rejoice over something.

If your ears burn, rub saliva on them and say:

> *Good, Good, Good betide them.*
> *Bad, Bad, May the devil ride them.*

SOURCES

1. Field Worker: Mrs. Rebecca Stonestreet. Washington. 1938. Field Worker: Harriett Hallworth.
2. Field Worker: Martha G. Bell. March, 1936.
3. Informant: Mrs. D. B. Price and Mrs. P. Newbern. Ocilla. Jan., 1936.
4. Informant: Mrs. Elizabeth Thompson. Atlanta. Field Worker: E. Driskell.

5. Field Worker: Louise McKinney. Fannin and Gilmer Counties. June, 1936.
6. Field Worker: Louise McKinney. Fannin and Gilmer Counties. June, 1936.
   Informant: George Leonard, ex-slave. Atlanta. Field Worker: Ed Driskell, 1936.
7. Field Worker: Edith Bell Love. Augusta, 1937.
8. Field Worker: Dorothy Plagwitz. Augusta. 1936.
9. Field Worker: J. R. Jones. Muscogee and Talbot Counties. 1936.
10. Informants: Mrs. Emmaline Heard, ex-slave and son Sid Heard. Field Worker: Minnie Roso.
    Informant: Hattie Taylor, ex-slave. Columbus. Field Worker: J. R. Jones. 1936.
    Field Worker: Marion Kumar, Albany 1937.
    Field Worker: Rebecca Stonestreet, Washington.

CHAPTER VI

FOLK WISDOM

Human Features, Proverbs, and Expressions

Few elements of folklore are as memorable for the people of Georgia as are the beliefs, proverbs, and expressions presented in this book. Except in extraordinary intellects men think and speak in cliches, and folk literature by definition is a collection of the commonplace. When one needs to express an emotion, make a comparison, or prove a point he turns to a form of phrasing he has heard before. The sunset is "as pretty as a picture," and the wife is "as busy as a beaver." When giving advice or commenting on the actions of others, we become the cliched moralist: "There is no fool like an old fool," and "Blood is thicker than water."

The sayings, proverbs, and beliefs included here are not peculiar to Georgia alone; however, they form a part of Georgia's past and present, and they were gleaned by field workers from every part of the state. Their wide use if not their absolute truth is clear. Mountain folk in North Georgia often will have no business dealings with a man whose beard is of a noticeably different color than his hair. Anywhere in the state a person with small ears is generally thought to be stingy, and full lips are always a sure sign of an affable and generous man.

Many of the sayings are variations from Shakespeare, Pope, the Bible, Franklin, or almanacs; others are anthropomorphisms. Georgians have altered the Biblical injuncion to "Before healing others, heal thyself." Often the changes simply reflect Georgia's basic agricultural economy. "If you eat dirt, be sure it's clean dirt." "Never tell the other fellow how to run his business; he will learn your trade secrets." "Corn earns more at the mill than in the crib." "When you remember the fate of the fattened hog you will be prosperous."

141

Often folk wisdom aims at expressing counsel or wisdom in a few words or a simple simile. Most important, however, it reveals that rural man is often a close observer of human nature.

H U M A N   F E A T U R E S[1]

The Body

Square athletic shoulders bespeak strength, pride, and vanity.

Broad shoulders and wide hips indicate great physical strength and endurance, especially when accompanied by bowlegs.

A disproportionately short-armed man has an inferior mentality.

Disporportionately long arms mean that their owner is a man of studious nature.

A man with a bull neck is one of dangerous passion.

A person who is knock-kneed is usually very strong.

If a man walks pigeon-toed, he won't pay his debts.

If a person has six fingers or toes, or other fancied resemblances to animals, his mother was frightened by an animal while she was pregnant.

Ears

Small ears that cling close to the head belong to a narrow-minded individual.

When the ears are small and flat, clinging closely to the head, they show selfishness.

Large ears show a generous nature.

When the ear lobe is large and thick it shows that the person's interests are large and varied.

Ears that stand out prominently mark their owner as generous.

Ears of any size set forward and extending outward mean a meddlesome person of little character.

The ear which stands out from the head indicates a love of music.

Long narrow ears show musical ability.

Small ears indicate sharpness of thought and glibness of speech.

Eyes

Medium sized eyes with thin lid and which have a dreamy expression indicate an idealistic temperament; such a person is highly emotional and very susceptible to beauty. In connection with high forehead and finely cut features, such eyes indicate creative ability.

A pop-eyed person is usually honest but seldom profound.

Round eyes denote an affectionate disposition, fidelity, faithfulness, loyalty, and filial devotion.

One with eyes that droop at the outer corners and a mouth of the same type is a person to stay away from.

A man whose eyes are set narrowly apart is a treacherous person.

Eyes which are long from side to side denote ambition, shrewdness, watchfulness, great secretiveness, and suspicion. The possessors are impulsive, impetuous, inclined to fickleness and are quick to recover from vicissitudes of any nature.

A man whose eyes are set wide apart is trustworthy and one whose eyes are close together is untrustworthy.

A squint-eyed person is close-fisted.

A moon-eyed individual is tricky.

A fish-eyed person has no ambition.

Large and open eyes denote development of the nerves of sensation. Those who possess them are sensitive, easily hurt and somewhat changeable, but kind-hearted and trustful.

A cross-eyed individual is often accused of having the evil-eye.

Deep-set eyes denote caution and prudence. If they have a penetrating expression the owner is strong-willed, determined, and inclined to be critical and domineering. Such a person is true and firm in friendship.

Large round eyes indicate love of literature and capacity for elocution, keen observation, fine discernment and social qualities.

A person whose eyebrows meet is mean and jealous.

Grey eyes reveal steadiness and poise and perhaps some coldness.

Black eyes belong to people who are emotional and cruel. Black eyes may flash with anger, envy and depth of feeling— either good or bad.

Grey-eyed people are the smartest and also the most dangerous.

Brown eyes denote affection, devotion, and mirth.

Hazel eyes indicate humor; however, they also reveal changeableness and sometimes instability.

Green eyes are intellectual and show suspicion and jealousy.

Blue-eyed people are the most honest and sincere.

Fingers

The fingernails are an index to character. Their care and appearance go far in indicating whether a person is honest or dishonest; temperate or intemperate; industrious or lazy; or artistic.

The longer the finger, the longer the fancy; the broader the finger, the broader the mind; the coarser the finger, the coarser the soul.

The shape of the hand and fingers and the lines in the hand reveal one's character.

Stubby fingers indicate a low grade of mentality.

Long, slender, beautiful fingers mark their owner as a potential musician, artist, idler, or dreamer. Such a person's occupation is dependent upon how he applies himself.

An unusually short little finger is a sign of some weakness of intellect *e.g.,* an inability to grasp details or to see the point of a joke.

A person with little fingers is a crook and a liar.

The shape of the thumb is most important.

A well-developed second joint of the thumb is proof of strength of character.

Index and third fingers of the same length denote an even, unexcitable temperament. If these two fingers vary radically in length, their possessor is erratic and flighty.

A person with long nails is philosophic, while one with short, broad nails is a person of physical strength.

Brittle nails are a sign of ill-health.

Ruddy nails indicate a healthy blood condition; white and bleached nails denote impoverished blood.

Bitten nails on a child indicate worry; bitten nails on a grown-up show a nervous temperament or one which is dyspeptic.

Thick nails denote common blood, birth and breeding.

Thin, transparent nails are a sign of an aristocrat.

The more pronounced the half-moons of nails, the more intelligent the individual.

A lunatic's nails are inclined to curl upward.

The nails of a moron have a tendency to curl downward.

The nails of dunces and idiots grow very slowly.

The faster the nails grow, the stronger and more active is the brain.

Talon-like nails are the sign of a selfish, greedy personality.

The Head

A head that is very wide at the ears with a narrow forehead and jaws means that its possessor would look out for Number One always.

Well filled-out temples are an evidence of intelligence.

A sloping forehead betrays animal qualities and degeneration.

A narrow-headed person is narrow-minded.

A high forehead and firm chin denote intelligence and strength of character.

A smooth forehead with a high crown indicates a generous and a reverent person, one who is good enough to be a preacher.

A high brow proclaims that one is intelligent.

One who habitually walks with his head bent forward and his eyes on the ground is one who would get what he could and keep what he got.

Baldness denotes wisdom.

High cheek bones denote a fiery temper.

A well-developed under-jaw and chin denote a bulldog tenacity—a person of moral and physical courage.

A receding chin indicates intellect, but also weak character.

A light beard is the result of fine breeding.

A dish-faced person is mean or tricky.

Hair

Red heads are "hot heads." They are argumentative and impatient of contradiction or restraint.

A person whose hair grows low on the forehead is usually idiotic.

If you cut your hair in the new moon it will grow faster.

Hands

"Snaky" hands indicate one is a thief or is not to be trusted.

A broad hand with short fingers, if the nails are not stubby, denotes executive ability.

One whose hand has a large palm and short fingers is perceptive and aware of the importance of details.

A long, narrow hand indicates musical ability.

The "spatulate" hand has wide finger ends and a broad base where the fingers join the hand. This shows much independence of spirit and is found among explorers, navigators, and engineers.

Lips

Thin lips are indicative of stinginess and selfishness.

A full lower lip with a wide mouth means an ardent lover and one who likes good food and good liquor, fast horses and pretty women.

A long upper lip indicates a liar and a treacherous person.

When the upper lip is long and the mouth shuts firmly, the owner is stubborn and never betrays a secret.

Full lips are a sign of an amiable and affectionate nature; but if too full they mean selfish indulgence.

Moles

A decided degree of success and prosperity follows the person who has a mole on his nose.

A mole on the cheek may comfort the individual who has one for he never will suffer from poverty or lack of friends, although he never will possess great wealth.

A mole at the corner of the eye indicates an industrious, reliable person, honest and pleasant.

A mole to the right of the brow or the temple foretells unexpected wealth and honor.

On the right eyebrow a mole foretells a youthful and happy marriage; should a mole appear to the left of the brow, eyebrow or temple, misfortune will bring sorrow and disappointment.

A person who has a mole on the left knee is hasty in his judgments, quick in temper, but honest and retiring on the whole. A mole on the right knee always indicates a person who need expect no overwhelming misfortunes or disappointment in life and who may look for happiness in his marital venture.

A person with a mole on the leg will prove lazy, inconsiderate and careless of consequences, while on the ankle it shows a man to be foppish and overly nice in his manners. The same mole on a woman's ankle means that she is brave, hot tempered and thrifty.

A mole anywhere on the ribs indicates that a person is a bit dull of comprehension and is unwilling to pursue his way should it be set with work and labor.

A mole on the left thigh denotes want of money and friends, while on the right thigh it denotes wealth and contentment in wedlock. Either of these moles shows fortitude and patience.

A mole on the stomach often indicates that an individual is lazy and greedy.

A round mole is good, an oval one means good fortune in moderation, while if square or jagged it denotes an even distribution of laughter and tears throughout your life.

A very hairy mole brings a good deal of bad luck, but one with no hair or only a few strands indicates a prosperous and contented life.

Nose

Regular features with a Roman nose indicate a good checker player; such a person could make four jumps and get a king but at the same time would bear watching.

A small nose curving inward and slightly upward to a point is an indication of inquisitiveness and of minding other folks' business.

A flat nose is a symbol of animalistic qualities.

A sharp-nosed person is stingy and would squeeze a dollar till the eagle hollered.

A Roman nose is the nose of a money lover.

A wart on the nose indicates too much curiosity.

Teeth

Even occlusion of the teeth is a sign of an unexcitable, phlegmatic temperament.

Upper teeth that overlap lower teeth indicate imagination.

Persons with gaps between their teeth are big liars.

Buck teeth denote mental derangement.

ADVICE AND BEHAVIOR[2]

A man who swears a little, drinks a little, and enjoys his pipe, his dog and his horse, can usually be trusted.

A man's pride doesn't count when he's dead.

Better the day—better the deed.

Before healing others, heal thyself.

A teacher who remains in one place longer than three years will not get married.

A tattling woman will make bread fall while it is baking.

Looks won't split rails.

While ghosts seldom bother an honest man, it is just as well to skirt the graveyard.

You can hide fire but smoke betrays you.

It's a very deaf person who fails to hear the dinner bell.

If you have to eat dirt, be sure it's clean dirt.

Lose no time; be always employed in something useful; cut off all unnecessary actions.

Corn earns more at the mill than in the crib.

A neighbor's tongue is a person's worst enemy.

Resolve to perform what you ought; perform without fail what you resolve.

Make no expense but to do good to other for yourself; waste nothing.

Never defeat one's self in order to defeat the other fellow.

Opportunity knocks but once at every man's door.

Use no hurtful deceit; think innocently and justly and, if you speak, speak accordingly.

Never cross a bridge before you get to it.

Eat not to dullness; drink not to elevation.

Two clean sheets can't smut, meaning a devout man or woman can't sin.

Be moderate in all things, especially drink and courtship, else you will be sorry in the future.

Let all your things have their place; let each part of your business have its time.

People who live in glass houses should not throw stones.

Speak not but what may benefit others or yourself; avoid trifling conversation.

Never tell the other fellow how to run his business, else he will learn your trade secrets.

Truth, though crushed to earth, shall rise again.

Whistling girls and crowing hens are sure to come to some bad end.

Better to play safe than to be sorry.

Idiots and fools do not sink or drown in the water.

ANIMALS

Remember the fate of the fattening hog when you are prosperous.

Don't expect rain every time a pig squeals.

A rain crow's voice is harsh, but you can depend on him to predict rain.

When a coon takes to water, he is ready for a fight.

A wise bee knows the sweetest honey is made from bitter flowers.

A blind horse doesn't fall when he follows the bit.

Don't plow with a racing mare.

If the mink knew where the dog sleeps, you'd see more of him.

A gray mare's funeral will bring all the buzzards around.

When the cat's away the mice will play.

A bird in the hand is worth two in the bush.

Dogs don't bite at the front gate.

Don't count your chickens before they hatch.

A howling dog knows what he sees.

A hungry rooster keeps quiet when he finds a worm.

A bird that sings too soon will be caught, so don't sing before breakfast.

Butter a cat's paw to keep him from leaving home.

More fun than a barrel of monkeys.

More fun than a mule can pull in a wagon.

As untrustworthy as a rainbow-faced horse.

Died a peckerwood death.

Handle like a cow tripe.

I've been here ever since Cooney was a kitten and he's now an old gray cat.

FOLK SPEECH COMPARISONS

Clever as a beaver.

Slow as Moses.

Sly as a weasel.

Dumb as an ox.

Big as an ox.

Cunning as a fox.

Thin as a razorback hog.

Big as a mite.

Strong as a mule.

Big as an elephant.

Poor as a snake.

Hot as a fox.

Weak as a kitten.

Bold as a lion.

Keen as a razor.

As right as rain.

As scared as turkey.

Hard as nails.

Pretty as a picture.

Smart as a whit.

Slow as Christmas.

Slick as a whistle.

Cold as blue blazes.

Green as a gourd.

Lonesome as a screech owl in a graveyard.

Thin as a razorback hog.

As natural as a pig in mud.

As happy as a jaybird after he's robbed a sparrow's nest.

As gay as a colt in a barley patch.

Just as thick as fleas on a dog's back.

Big as a bale of cotton.

Sorry as gulley dirt.

Just as natural as life.

Thick as peas in a pod.

Slow as molasses in winter.

Hot as a June bride.

Hot as hell.   Cold as hell.   Big as hell.   Mean as hell.

EXPRESSIONS[3]

Come in and sit a spell.

Old man Know-All died last year.

Still waters run deep.

A rolling stone gathers no moss.

What goes in by one ear goes out by the other.

Too many hands spoil the pudding.

I'll do thus and so when I get "recruited up"
(meaning recovered).

Looks like a million dollars.

When in anger count to ten;
when very angry count to one hundred.

Nothing rattles like an empty wagon.

Spare the rod and spoil the child.

Idleness is the devil's workshop.

You can put it in your pipe and smoke it.

Hard work never hurt anybody.

A guilty conscience cries aloud.

I wouldn't trust him from shirt tail to bed time.

Whiskey and gasoline don't mix.

Whiskey and women will ruin any man.

As certain as death and taxes.

Don't kick a man when he's down.

As sure as you're living.

As sure as I'm standing here.

He's a regular mountain rooter.

Too slow to catch cold.

The big bad wolf will get you.

Slowpoke, come on!

Making a mountain out of a mole-hill.

Cut up like a Friday fool.

That's a horse of another color.

Speak of the devil and look who appears.

Swallow it hook, line and sinker.

Take it with a grain of salt.

I'm fixin' to go.

The Lord takes care of fools and drunkards.

No news is good news.

There ain't no if's, and's, or but's about it.

Time and tide wait for no man.

An apple a day keeps the doctor away.

Every dog has his day.

Waste not, want not.

A bad penny always turns up.

Curiosity killed the cat.

Beauty is only skin deep.

He may be gone but not forgotten.

He who laughs last laughs best.

Easy come, easy go.

A new broom sweeps clean.

Charity begins at home.

Blood is thicker than water.

Good riddance to bad rubbish.

Good, better, best, never let it rest,
till the good is better and the better is best.

Finders keepers, losers weepers.

It never rains but it pours.

Give the cow a lick of salt to catch the calf.

Leave well enough alone.

No rest for the wicked.

Let a sleeping dog lie.

Children are to speak only when spoken to.

It takes two to tango.

There is more than one way to skin a cat.

You can't have your cake and eat it too.

If the shoe fits, wear it.

Hell is paved with good intentions.

Don't put off until tomorrow what you can do today.

Honesty is the best policy.

Pert as can be.

Just keep your shirt on.

Laugh fit to kill.

Makin' glory hump.

Looking like butter won't melt in his mouth.

Easy as falling off a log.

There aren't any two ways about it.

There was a heap more under his hat
than you could get out with a fine tooth comb.

There wouldn't have been enough of him left
for the congregation to sing a song over.

He wasn't as big as a pound of soap
after a hard day's washing.

Bloody bones will get you.

Red eyes will get you.

Like a streak of greased lightning.

Chip off the old block.

Happy is the bride that the sun shines on.

It takes two birds to make a nest.

You never pay for your raising
until you raise a family of your own.

OLD-TIME NEGRO EXPRESSIONS[4]

Walking with the boys. (An expression used to denote that a young Negro girl has begun to receive male company.)

Holding hands.
(to become engaged).

I've got religion.
(To have become converted).

Into hell he leaped.
(He died unrepentant and unsaved)

Got hisself up.
(Bettered his condition; acquired property.)

Stuck his head in a halter.
(Got married)

Jumped over the broomstick.
(She got married.)

Did fetchingly well.
(Did exceedingly well.)

The bottom rail got on top.
(A once-poor man who has prospered.)

I tell you what Gods knows.
(To tell the solemn truth.)

Brotherhooded.
(To be framed or conspired against in a noncriminal
but unethical way.)

Railroaded.
(To become the victim of a criminal conspiracy.)

Feathered his nest.
(Looked to his own interests.)

Walked George and went South.
(Stole something and ran away.)

Two streaks of rust and a right-o-way.
(Contemptuous expression for a jerk-water railroad.)

Burned his bridges behind him.
(Severed all ties and connections.)

Got his duster fanned.
(Received a beating.)

Fouled his nest. (One who has proved untrue to a trust, or by some indiscreet act or word, has courted public disfavor.)

Pulled off his shirt.
(Did his level best.)

Ran with the hounds and played with the hares. (Played fast and loose with friends, associates, or colleagues.)

MISCELLANEOUS PROVERBS AND EXPRESSIONS[5]

Cut your fingernails on Monday, you cut them for news.
Cut them on Tuesday, get a new pair of shoes.
Cut them on Wednesday, you cut them for wealth.
Cut them on Thursday, you cut them for health.
Cut them on Friday, you cut them for sorrow;
Cut them on Saturday, see your sweetheart tomorrow;
Cut them on Sunday, its safety you seek;
But the devil will have you the rest of the week.

Sneeze on Monday, you are in danger.
Sneeze on Tuesday, kiss a stranger.
Sneeze on Wednesday, sneeze for a letter.
Sneeze on Thursday, something better.
Sneeze on Friday, sneeze for sorrow.
Sneeze on Saturday, see your beau tomorrow.
Sneeze on Sunday, safety seek;
    the devil will have you the rest of the week.

Some men's brains would rattle in a mustard seed like a buckshot in a coffee pot.

Some babbling tongues, like Tennyson's brook, run on forever.

Better be gravy than no grease at all.

Fools' names, like fools' faces, are often seen in public places.

Moonshine won't take the place of lightwood knots.

Sleeping in fence corners will rob Christmas in the house.

Don't measure my quart by your half bushel.

SOURCES

1. Taken from reports submitted by J. R. Jones, W. C. Massey and Lila Ellis, Field Workers. 1936, 1937.
2. Field Worker: LeGarde S. Doughty. Augusta. 1937.
3. Field Worker: Dorothy Plagwitz. Augusta. 1937.
4. Field Worker: J. R. Jones. Muscogee and Talbot Counties. 1937. Notation on top of list reads "From personal knowledge."
5. Informant: Fran Avery. Rome. April, 1937.

CHAPTER VII

BELIEFS AND CUSTOMS:
MAN AND HIS ENVIRONMENT

(Weather, Animals, Farming, Planting, Fishing, Hunting)

A profusion of folk beliefs concerning man and his environment circulate in Georgia, many of which, like the proverbs and tales, reflect an agricultural economy. This folk wisdom, of course, even tempered men's attitudes toward each other. It is natural in fox-hunting country, for example, that a man who doesn't make friends with dogs should be regarded as a suspicious character.

The folk beliefs in this collection reveal more than any other form of folklore the basic everyday life patterns of white and black Georgians throughout the history of the state. Other forms are more exotic, but none has been more universally known and followed. The number of conjure doctors was never great; Georgia's population always has been composed of farm families whose livelihood depended upon their knowledge of the environment. It mattered to the farmer that he could read the signs or plan for the seasons by knowing nature's signals.

Many of these folk beliefs have their origin in the nature religions of Africa and were brought to Georgia with the slaves, but Christian symbols have all but erased the original African Spirits.

The distinction between fact and superstition is more difficult to determine in folk belief than elsewhere in folk literature. A crimson sunset may indeed foretell a summer shower, but one wonders about the aching of corns or the screaming of a peacock. Zoologists verify the truth of numerous folk beliefs about animals, but there are those who doubt that bees will not cross a stream to gather nectar, or that all animals kneel at the stroke of midnight on Christmas eve.

All of these beliefs show the rural Georgian as possessing an imaginative and creative mind, but primarily they reveal his intelligence in observing nature and his success in achieving accommodation to his environment.

WEATHER[1]
(Signs, Lightning, Rain, Superstitions)

SIGNS

When hogs begin making a bed of leaves, that means cold weather.

It is a good sign of cold, windy weather when pigs begin to run and squeal.

Thick corn shucks predict a cold, hard winter.

The butterfly flying southward foretells an early winter.

It is a sign of freezing weather when great numbers of birds gather around a house.

An abundance of fruit and nuts indicates a severe winter, and *vice versa*.

A squirrel gathering acorns before they are ripe predicts a cold, hard winter.

Look out for a hard winter when 'coons have a heavy growth of fur, chipmunks and squirrels are busier than usual, insects leave the north side of trees, feathers on geese are thicker than usual, young lambs grow heavy fleeces, and sheared sheep regain their wool in a short time.

When birds come in large numbers close to the house it is a sign of freezing weather.

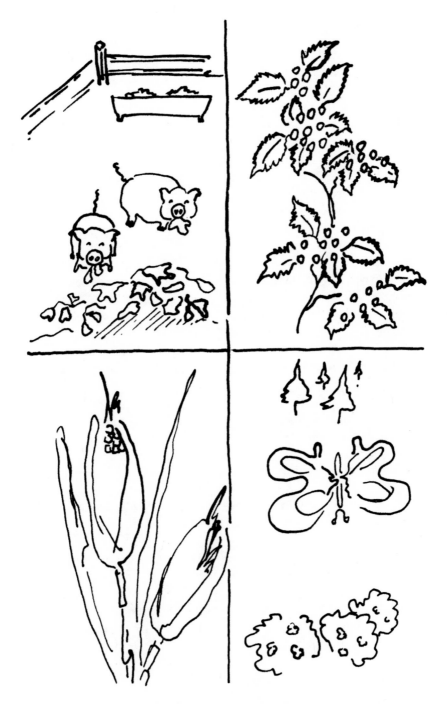

Signs Of A Cold Winter

When holly and mistletoe have a lot of berries there will be a cold, hard winter.

It will be ninety days until the first frost after the first July fly (cicada) cries in the summer.

When a yellow-hammer sings, warm weather is due; the cooing of a dove means clear weather; when the whipporwill cries, there is to be no more frost.

The cawing of crows is a good omen and foretells the approach of Indian Summer.

The arrival of woodpeckers is a sign of spring. They come south by night and go north by day.

Lightning

Lightning in the North at night indicates rain within twenty-four hours.

Lightning in the East never brings a feast; lightning in the West is a sign of the best.

Lightning never strikes a sycamore, the tree being blessed.

The Cherokees believed that any tree struck by lightning, especially if it were alive, had mysterious properites.

If seeds are placed in water in which lightning-struck wood is soaked, the crop will be bountiful.

When charcoal made from lightning-struck wood is rubbed on ball players' hands it gives them power to strike a ball with the force of a thunderbolt.

RAIN

Signs of Rain

If corns on feet hurt
If broken bones ache.
If one dreams of the dead.
If frogs croak.
If the sun sets in big, red clouds.
Rheumatic pains.
Thunderheads in the north in summer time.
Distant lightning in the north.
If noses itches.
If goblets or glasses filled with cold water sweat.
If a peacock screams.

If the sun sets behind a bank of clouds on Sunday afternoon, there will be rain before Wednesday night, and if the sun sets behind a bank of clouds on Wednesday afternoon, there will be rain before Sunday.

> An evening gray and a morning red
> Send the shepherd wet to bed.
> An evening red and morning gray—
> Two sure signs of one fine day.

A horse with an unusually fluffy mane and tail portends rain within twenty-four hours.

If a tree frog croaks in a tree in the day time, rain will come within the next two or three days.

When clouds obscure the sun, rain is assured for next day.

Rain often follows a big frost.

A bank of clouds across the north late of an evening is another wet-weather sign.

Kill a spider and rain will come.

Flies in the house are an indication of rain.

The cry of a rain crow after a drought is a sure sign of rain.

Sometimes the air feels hard and dry, and at such times the weather will be dry. If, however, the air feels damp there will soon be rain.

If the sun sets in red clouds it is the sign of rain.

A summer sun setting behind a bank of clouds is a sign of rain.

A halo around the moon and a crimson sunset both indicate bad weather.

If a star is near the moon, or within a ring around the moon, it will rain shortly.

A sure sign of rain is to see "water dog" (rainbow 1 ft. to 6 ft. long) either to right or left of the sun late in the afternoon.

Rattling of leaves in tree tops on hot, still nights is another sure sign of rain.

When fish run upstream, it is a sign of rain. When they travel downstream, it is a sign of approaching drought.

If flies bite you it is a sign of rain.

If smoke goes to the ground it is a sign of rain.

If your head itches it is going to rain.

It will rain in May for each time it thunders in February.

A rain beginning before seven will cease before eleven.

If it rains while the sun is shining, it will rain at the same time the next day.

The moon affects rainfall. There is more rain when the moon is changing in the evening—that is, waning, quartering, and the like, than when it is changing in the morning.

A morning rain is like an old maid's dancing; it soon gives out.

If it rains on the day of a wedding bad luck will attend the couple.

If you kill a snake and hang it over a fence, rain will fall within twenty-four hours.

If you are in need of rain invite the circus to town.

If you prepare yourself for rain by carrying an umbrella it will certainly not rain.

If it rains while the sun is shining the devil is beating his wife.

During a thunderstorm the angels are moving their furniture around in heaven.

Stepping on ants brings rain.

Rain the first five days of the week means clearing weather by Friday.

When the sky is very blue rain will soon follow, and when dry leaves are seen whirling and dancing in circles, the weather will change.

Catch the first May shower and you will be well all spring.

If rain falls on the first of Dog Days (July 3 to August 11), it will fall every day throughout the period. If the first day is fair, fair weather will prevail.

If the weather clears during the night, rain will follow within twenty-four hours.

Wind

The East wind incites peevishness, rheumatism, and grumbling, and curls one up in the chimney corner.

The West wind is peaceful and harmonious and is an effeminate suggestion of luxurious ease.

The North wind is uplifting and bracing, and puts the stamina of endurance into a man.

The South wind is soft and soothing, and fans the wayward mind gently to sleep.

Rainbow

The Cherokee Indians believed if you point at the rainbow your finger will swell at the lower joint.

Both ends of the rainbow terminate in the ocean.

> *Rainbow in the morning, sailors's warning*
> *Rainbow in the night, sailor's delight.*

Follow the rainbow to the end and find a pot of gold.

Snow

When it snows the angels are picking geese.

When it snows the angels are having a pillow fight.

A singing fire is a sign of snow.

The gathering of grouse into large flocks indicates snow.

A N I M A L S[2]

Cats

It is bad luck to kill a cat.

If a strange cat comes to your house, you will have good luck.

It is unlucky to move cats from one house to another.

A cat should never sleep near a child as it will suck the child's breath.

Black cats are sometimes witches, and if you rub the fur of a black cat at night you will see the sparks of fire it has brought from hell.

Never give a black cat away; lend it, or you'll have bad luck.

A cat brushing against one's leg, and purring softly as it does so denotes a change in the weather.

A cat can cause the death of a sleeping person by sucking his breath.

If a black cat crosses your path, turn back or you will have bad luck; or you may go on if you take off your hat and spit in it.

If you are the first person that a cat looks at after he has licked himself, you are going to be married.

If you put a kitten under the cover of your bed and leave it until it crawls out, it will never leave home.

Reptiles

A king snake is immune to the poisons of all venomous snakes.

A rattlesnake is stone deaf; also, if exposed to 85° of sun heat, it will die within fifteen minutes.

The white oak or tree snake has four feet.

It brings good luck to kill the first snake you see in spring; if you burn the snake near the house no mice will come about the premises.

When camping, draw a ring with a sharp stick around the tent; snakes will not cross the mark. A rope around the tent answers the same purpose.

The coach whip, a Southern black snake of the boa-constrictor family, often milks cows.

If a coach whip snake catches your eyes it will fascinate you into helplessness by its gaze, wrap itself about you, and tickle you to death.

It is believed that a coach whip snake will chase a person until he is caught; then it proceeds to whip the person until he is dead. After the person has been whipped for some time, the snake then determines whether he is dead by putting his head in the whipped person's nose. If breathing has stopped the snake will go its way.

A snake tail will not die until sundown.

If you kill a snake and put it in the fire its feet and legs will come out from under its scales.

A bull snake bellows like a bull.

Before hibernating for the winter, alligators swallow large quantities of pine knots.

No snake and no turtle, regardless of the time of day when it is killed, will die until sundown.

No poisonous snake or skunk will cross a hair rope.

Birds

When a screech owl screams it is the sign of death. To stop him from screaming turn your left-hand pants pocket wrong side out or take off the left shoe and turn the sole up or turn your apron inside out; failing in this, throw a coal of fire out of a window.

To kill an owl, walk around the tree several times. He will keep turning his head to watch you until he twists if off.

To stop a screech owl put a shovel in a hot bed of embers.

Owls may be driven away by throwing salt on a fire. Also, a woman's shoe placed in a corner of the room will make an owl fly away.

If a buzzard files over your house, you will get a letter or hear good news.

When crows congregate in great numbers and hold court, look for a change in the weather.

It is unlucky to shoot or cripple a bird and then let it die in your hand.

It is bad luck to shoot a robin, good luck to put out food for it.

When swallows are very active on the wing, the wind will soon blow hard.

If a bird or bat falls down the chimney, someone in the house is going to die within six months.

Sprinkling salt on a bird's tail will prevent its flying away.

Buzzards circling over a community signify that a funeral is soon to be held.

Jay birds are never seen on Friday. On that day they go to hell, each taking a grain of sand to place on the fire. After taking its quota of sand, each bird becomes free from the danger of hell fire.

Chickens

When chickens flock and are very quiet and inactice, a change of weather will soon follow.

Rooster crowing in front of house means company is coming. If it crows at midnight, it is a sign of bad luck. Crowing at dusk means rain in the morning.

If a wet hen and a wet dog have a collision, a flood and a storm will follow.

Put a rusty nail in chicken water to make the fowl tender. Or take a broken plate and cook the chicken in the pot to tenderize it.

Cows

When a cow's blood becomes impoverished and its health is shattered as a consequence, nature sends a tick to purify the animal's blood. Therefore, it is wrong to kill cow ticks.

If a cow's horns are to be cut off, a time should be selected when the zodiac sign is in her feet or some other place than the head.

To cure hollowtail in cattle, split the tail near the body and pour in salt and pepper.

A big-footed cow has large bones and makes tough beef.

A long-headed steer makes the most valuable and intelligent work-ox.

When a cow gets sick through losing her cud, wind a ball of wool thread tightly and fry it in hot lard and make her swallow it.

Red cows are the gentlest.

If an ox and a horse are harnessed together, one will die, because Moses forbade yoking the ox and ass together.

The heifer twin of a bull calf will not reproduce.

To milk a cow on the ground will cause her to go dry, unless you throw some of the milk on her back.

If a calf is born on Sunday, its mother will be a good milch cow.

Calves born during winter months are hardy, but make smaller cattle than those born in other seasons.

Cowhide is the best leather because it is non-porous. A cow never sweats, except through the glands of the nose.

If a man drinks beef blood, it will make him fierce and strong.

Dogs

A dog sweats only at his nose, and fleas on him have to go to his nose for water; therefore, a greasy collar placed around a dog's neck will kill all fleas behind the collar as they visit the dog's nose to quench their thirst.

Dogs having pointed, upright ears are representatives of vicious types.

Never trust any dog that doesn't yawn occasionally.

Dogs whelped inside a sheep lot will make good sheep dogs.

Flop-eared dogs, as a rule, are friendly.

When a pet dog lies down in the middle of the road and howls at the moon, somebody in his owner's house will shortly die.

Break green gourds over a dog's head to make him bark up a tree.

If you wish your dog or a cock to be vicious, feed it raw meat or other food sprinkled with gunpowder.

An onion rubbed over a dog's nose will stop him from hunting, and he will trail nothing.

To prevent a hunting dog from running spirits, i.e. chasing ghosts, tie a glass button around the dog's neck.

To keep a strange dog with you, cut some hair off the end of his tail and bury it under your doorstep.

Dogs smell death. A dog leaves its master when all hope of recovery is gone and flees in terror before the presence of death.

When a dog throws his head up in the air and sniffs, he is smelling rain.

When a dog travels on three legs he is adding the days until it rains.

Dogs bay at the man in the moon and at spirits; sometimes they seem to bay the old moon out and the new moon in.

In antebellum days slaves believed that any solid black dog could, by urinating on a gate post or door step, make the owner thereof a blood cousin to the dog's owner.

Hogs

There is something perculiar about a hog's vision that enables it to see the wind. He's seen it when he squeals.

When a hog and a cow form an affinity, as they often do on farms, it is bad luck to separate them.

The eye-tooth of a hog worn around one's neck makes a good charm to ward off evil spirits.

It takes more corn to fatten a long-legged hog than it does a short-legged one. The long-legged hog trots off his fat.

The best brood sows are those which will leave an ear of corn to eat a handful of acorns.

Kill hogs on the increase of the moon to make the carcasses weigh more. Killing on the wane of the moon causes the meat to shrink.

A hog's sense of smell is as acute as that of a dog. A hog can trail a man better than the average dog can, provided the trail is not over two hours old.

To select a good boar for a stock hog, pick one that is a good rooter.

To induce a sow to breed, feed her cracklings (the residue of rendered hog lard).

A long-snouted hog will eat chickens.

Hogs confined in a pen warn of an approaching blizzard by their nervous action and squealing.

Horses

Tie a small piece of deer horn to a colt's mane and he will have speed.

Stamp one of your palms for each white horse you see and when you get to a hundred you will find something.

If you walk through a place where a horse wallows you will have a headache.

A multi-colored horse has the greatest intelligence.

All colts born in the month of May will lie down in water when in harness or under the saddle.

A vicious horse or mule always throws back his ears before attacking.

A rabbit-breasted horse has the best wind.

The fastest horses have short backs and long barrels.

A young horse, depending upon his size, type and breeding, is worth $50 or $100 for each roll-over he makes while wallowing.

White horses can endure great heat but are unfit for mountain use because their hoofs are tender. Black horses cannot stand great heat but can endure terrific cold. Sorrel horses have tender skins and suffer more than any others from thorns, briars and insects. A bay combines more ideal features than any other horse.

Horses and mules display more than usual liveliness and energy just before a rain.

A horse or mule will die of thirst rather than drink water in which a coon has bathed.

To make a balky horse go, tie a corn cob in his ear or twist his nose.

Flea-bitten gray horses and mules are usually spirited.

Place a chicken in a nervous horse's stall and let it roost there, and the horse will soon become calm.

Moon-eyed horses are not trustworthy.

A zebra-legged mule is always a game, hardy animal, possessed of unusual strength and endurance.

A horse runs away from what he hears; a mule runs away from what he sees; hence, open bridles are used for horses and blind bridles for mules.

A horse's baby teeth disappear at the age of four.

The eyes on horses' and mules' fore-legs were put there by nature to enable them to see better at night.

If a horse has one stocking-foot, deny him; two stocking feet, try him; three or four stocking feet, buy him.

Miscellaneous Animals and Insects

If you kill ants, the rest of the colony will begin to dig your grave.

When ant hills are high early in the morning, it is a sign of a fine day.

When ants are unusually busy, the weather will be stormy. Combat between swarms of ants presages war.

Ants never sleep.

Ants travel in lines before bad weather; when they travel separately the weather will continue fair.

The meanest of all varmits is the otter because he beats his wife three times a day.

The dumbest of all reptiles is the turtle. If one is basking on a log or stump when a shower starts, he will drop off into lake, pond or stream to avoid the raindrops.

An animal should never be operated upon when the sign of the zodiac is in the portion of its body that is to undergo surgery; otherwise profuse bleeding will follow.

Animals breeding on high ground produce tall offspring. When they breed in bottoms and lowlands, their progeny are low and chunky.

Animals can talk at midnight on Christmas Eve.

Black spots on the gills of the haddock were made by St. Peter with his finger and thumb when he took the tribute money out of the mouth of the fish.

The fish with which Jesus fed the multitude was the sea bass, and the black spots on this fish are the marks of His fingers, proving that Sweet Jesus was black.

Fur-bearing animals must be skinned in months spelled with an *r* in the name, and only in such months should oysters be eaten.

A swarm of bees in May is worth a load of hay.

A swarm in June is worth a silver spoon.

A swarm in July is not worth a fly.

Bees are supposed to sting an unchaste woman.

Bees are said to have originated in Paradise and to have come to earth for the sin of man; for that reason, the service of the Mass cannot be performed without lighting tapers made of their wax.

Bees will not cross a stream to gather nectar.

Bees early at work will not perform a full day's work.

Bees will not swarm before a coming storm.

The Lord made the sheep, but the Devil seeing it tried to make something like the sheep but failed, so he called it a goat.

If a he-goat sheds his whiskers in his owner's back yard, sickness will soon overcome some member of that man's family.

If you kill a frog, warts will come on your hand.

A turtle or crawfish will not let go until it thunders.

A snapping turtle, though its head be cut off, will return to water from a distance of a mile or two. Also, if a snapping turtle bites a man it will not let go of him until thunder is heard.

Alligators are fond of dogs and Negro children.

Spots peculiar to certain fish were put there by the devil, who in counting the fish occasionally hit them with his tail.

Any stream of water flowing at a rate of five miles an hour or greater purifies itself. Therefore, any fish or animal inhabiting it is clean and fit for food.

FARM WISDOM AND SUPERSTITIONS[3]

Soap is made more quickly and is of better quality when it is stirred with a sassafras stick.

Pigs, calves, and chickens born in the sign of the Scorpion or at the time of the new moon will die.

Clothes being washed in a stream cleanse more readily when whipped with a hickory stick.

Drinking water tastes better when served out of a cedar bucket or a long-handled gourd dipper.

Hickory ashes are the best for making lye, because they contain more potash than the ash of other woods.

Butterbean hulls must not be burned or fed to cattle or hogs but thrown into the road in order to insure the fertility of fields, cattle, hogs, and wife.

Hold the mouth full of water while peeling onions and the onion juice will not get in the eyes.

Put a horseshoe in the fire; as long as it remains red-hot hawks will not bother your chickens.

To insure an abundant corn crop, bury in the corn field cobs from which seed corn has been shelled. If the cobs are burned the crop will be burned by drought.

Pine wood cut in the first quarter of the moon will show more resin, dry better, and burn quicker.

If you want a hen to hatch only pullets, put under her eggs held in the bonnet of a girl.

To make a scarecrow more effective, cut its arms from a hickory tree.

If you carry seeds in your pocket, be sure there is no hole; else they will drop out and a bad crop will result.

Underground water may be found by walking around with a light willow twig held horizontally in the hand. When you come to a spot under which there is water, the ends of the twig will droop.

Mistletoe is said to have been created by the falling tears of Venus when she was wounded accidentally by one of Cupid's arrows.

It is unlucky to eat mulberries because the Devil uses them to black his boots.

It is unlucky to eat twin nuts in one shell. Give one to somebody else.

When oak trees bend in January, good crops may be expected.

Oak and walnut cannot stand together without one perishing. When oaks bear queer leaves, it is a forewarning of death or catastrophe.

Good luck will result from burying green persimmons.

Make a wish before you eat a pomegranate and the wish will come true.

Eat the eyes of a potato to overcome an enemy. You can then see what he is going to do.

Put a white flint rock in the fire and hawks will not catch your chickens.

To prevent a fall while walking on a log from one side of a creek to the other, place a small stick crosswise in the front teeth and no mishap will result.

PLANTING[4]

All things that mature above the ground, such as peas, corn, *etc.*, must be planted when the moon is passing from new to full. All things that mature under the soil, like potatoes, turnips, *etc.*, must be planted in the decrease or wane of the moon, while it passes from full to new.

If you wish okra to stop growing at a convenient height for picking, bend your body low when planting. It will make the plant grow fuller and not so tall.

For an abundant crop, butterbeans should be planted on Good Friday.

All plants with eyes, like potatoes, beans, peas, *etc.*, must be underground on Good Friday, or they will weep for the crucifixion.

Five grains of corn should be planted to each hill:

> *One for the hoe,*
> *One for the crow,*
> *One for the cut-worm,*
> *And two for to grow.*

In setting out cabbage plants, if you pinch off the tap root the plant will not go to seed.

Vegetables planted on the zodiacal sign of twins will be more prolific.

Plant corn on or after the full moon for abundant fruit. Planting on the moon's increase will cause most of the growth to go to stalk.

Plant watermelons, cucumbers, and cantaloupes on a waning moon.

Fall turnips may be planted immediately after dog days end.

If the ground hog sees his shadow on February Second, plant corn when the plum trees bloom; otherwise, wait until the first whippoorwill is heard. Late corn, however, can be planted in early July.

For a larger crop of vegetables that multiply, plant them when the zodiac sign is the arm.

Peas must be sown on Wednesday or Saturday; otherwise birds will carry them off.

Plant peppers when you are mad. It takes a high-tempered person to raise fine peppers.

If you plant onions over Irish potatoes, the potatoes will not suffer for moisture, as the onions will get in their eyes and thereby furnish water for both vegetables.

Plant cucumbers between 11 and 12 o'clock when the zodiac sign is in the arm.

The first love-apples (tomatoes) were poisonous, and grew out of ground where illicit lovers had been buried after having first been murdered or executed.

Vegetables such as peanuts and potatoes must be planted when the sign is in the arms (Gemini). Onions should be planted when the sign is in the Reins (Libra) so they will attain full weight. Whenever possible tomatoes, beans, and corn should be planted on the new of the moon and when the tips point upward so it will hold a bountiful quantity.

If you steal a flower and plant it, it will grow.

If one plants or cans beans when the zodiac signs are in the bowels, they will cause dysentery when eaten.

Whoever plants a cedar tree that lives, will not live long.

Plant a weeping willow tree and when it gets large enough to shade a grave, someone in the family will die.

In sowing cabbage seed, ignore the moon and follow the signs given in connection with the nude man in the almanac whose stoical countenance betrays neither pain nor concern over his laid-open bowels. Sow while the signs are in the head for either early or fall cabbage.

Plant cucumber seed while the signs are in the twins, if you want a larger yield.

While sweet potatoes may be planted at any time, put out Irish potatoes when the signs are in the thighs, for good smooth potatoes. If the signs are in the feet, the potatoes will have little horns and knobs scattered about their surface.

Sow cabbage seed on the old side of the moon. This causes straight cabbage stalks. If you sow seed on the new of the moon, there won't be a straight plant in the bed. And when plants have crooked stems, you can't tell how to get'em out. You can't place 'em right because you can't tell where their roots are.

Plant corn in April, May or any month you choose, but be sure you plant it after the full moon of the month chosen. Then the stalks will grow short and bear ears low and full. If you plant before the full of the moon, the stalks will grow too tall and the ears will stick up too straight.

Plant beans when the signs are in the feet. If you plant them when the signs are in the head, beans will appear halfway up the vines. Plant in the feet and the bean pods will spring out all the way up and down the length of the vine.

Sow pepper seed on the new of the moon and in three or four days the seed will all be spread on top of the ground.

Plant beets on the old of the moon. If you plant them on the new, they will grow sticking halfway out of the ground.

FISHING[5]

It is good luck to place elm leaves in the bait can or box.

It is good luck to put molasses or honey in the bait can.

Asafetida on the bait attracts fish.

Never go fishing on a full moon; always pick your time just before the full or just after it.

> *Wind from the east, fish bite least;*
> *Wind from the west, fish bite best;*
> *Wind from the south blows hook out of mouth;*
> *Wind from the north, don't bite at all.*

Never change poles if you catch a fish with the one you start out with.

Never change your hook if you have snared a fish on the one you are using.

It is bad luck to select a pole with long joints; good luck to use a pole whose joints are short.

The presence on the water of the mellow bug, a harmless insect black on top and yellow on the lower part of his body, shows where the fish are biting.

The best bait for fish is fresh meat, catawba worms, earth worms, pieces of fish, live minnows, or bacon.

"Hauling the seine" was a method of fishing in which a net varying in length from 6 to about 15 feet, with a staff affixed to one end, was dragged through the water. It was often done in pools below dams while the mill was grinding corn or wheat.

Brush-dragging was a procedure to stretch the seine across the stream and drag a treetop from the boiling pool at the dam to the stream proper, where it would float with the increased current. It was necessary for a couple of light men to ride the brush to keep it down on the bed of the stream and drive the fish into the seine. The brush often turned and dumped the riders into the stream.

It is lucky for a fisherman to get his feet wet, but unlucky for him to step on his line.

It is bad luck to throw back the little ones until your fishing is over.

Never allow fishing poles to cross; it means bad fishing luck.

Spitting on the bait will insure a good catch.

HUNTING[5]

Never hunt a 'possum on a moonlight night. Only the little ones are out with the moon. The best time to hunt 'possums is on a cloudy night just before the break of day. All of the big ones are out then.

When hunting in a swamp at night, if you run into a warm air current it is a sign you have come near a grave and its ghost is after you. To drive away the ghost, run your hand 'round and 'round over your face.

Never hunt at night in the vicinity of a cemetery. If you do, the dogs will give up the animal and chase ghosts.

Shooting birds before breakfast means a poor day's hunting.

Shooting the tail off a bird without otherwise injuring it is a warning to stop hunting the rest of the day under hazard of an accident.

Never carry shells in the left pocket unless you have some in other pockets too.

The "barking" of a squirrel by expert riflemen of many years ago was a fine art. The idea was to bring the squirrel down without drawing blood. This was done by super-creasing the squirrel—that is, by shocking it into insensibility and thereby causing it to fall.

Many an old timer would not shoot at a squirrel in the top of a very tall tree, for fear of "straining" his gun.

When you go rabbit hunting, pull out the tail of the first rabbit you kill, and you will see plenty more.

Turkey

The only way to get close enough to the wild turkey to shoot it is to imitate the call of another turkey. There are many devices for imitating the call of the turkey. One of the oldest is to take the small bone of a turkey wing and a piece of slate in a small, thoroughly-seasoned, hand-made box, about five inches long and one and one-half inches square, containing a piece of slate for the top. The slate projects a little and the noise is made by rubbing still a smaller piece of slate across the projecting edge.

Wolf Pit[6]

A round ditch was dug about six feet wide, several feet deep—say ten or twelve feet. In the center the earth was left undisturbed. A very high fence was built around this ditch, except at one place which was left low enough to allow a wolf to jump over it. In front of this low place the ditch was covered with light brush, straw, *etc.*, to look very much like the surrounding earth. In front of this low place in the fence and directly in front of the covering and straw over the ditch, on the ground in the center was placed the bait for the wolf, which was usually a sheep or a calf. Before placing the bait on the undisturbed spot in the center, someone would take the dead calf or sheep and drag it all around for some distance from the pit—like they do in fixing for a drag race—so the wolves would smell the blood and track along until they got to the pit. And upon reaching the fence at the pit the wolf would jump right over it, not suspecting the ditch he would fall into in attempting to reach the bait, and would land upon the straw-covered ditch and fall through to the bottom, and of course he could not get out. When his captors arrived, they would find him confined in the ditch and he would be quickly killed with a gun.

A RURAL VOCABULARY OF ANIMAL AND PLANT NAMES[7]

Ananias Hen.   A hen that cackles but doesn't lay; a lying hen.

Bait.   Any kind of angle worm.

Biddie.   A baby chicken.

Blue Bottle-fly.   A green blowfly that feeds on carrion.

Blue Darter.   A species of hawk.

Blue Snake.   A very large black snake of the boa constrictor family, reputed to attain a length of 15 feet.

Bullises.   Wild muscadines.

Belly Busters.   Bull-frogs, so-called because of their habit of leaping precipitately into water when frightened or disturbed.

Bear Grass.   A genus of flowering palmetto.

Candle-fly.   A genus of flowering palmetto.

Coach Whip.   A Southern black snake of the boa constrictor family.

Craw Dad.   Fresh-water crayfish.

Cribber.   A horse or mule that eats wood.

Dirt Dauber.   The mason wasp.

Doodle Bug.   The ant-lion.

Drunkards.   Minute, gnat-like insects which breed in exposed vinegar and cider containers, wine casks, etc.

Devil's Horse.   The praying mantis.

Deacon.   An orphan colt; also the hide of an unborn calf.

Ear Wig.	Any worm, large or small, that resembles a centipede.
Free Martin.	The twin sister of a bull calf. Free martins are rare and it is said that they are sterile.
Fresh Water Stingaree	A large black water bug that neither stings nor bites.
Frog Stool.	Any inedible, mushroom-like growth.
Goober.	A peanut
Gyp.	A female dog, fox, or wolf.
Google Eye.	A large-mouthed, yellow perch.
Ground-Puppy.	The spotted salamander; also a newt.
Gopher.	A common name given to several species of Southern land terrapins.
Grancy Graybeard	A weed, used in compounding some home medicines.
Ground Squirrel.	In Georgia, a chipmunk.
Horny Head.	A small fish of the sucker family.
Horned Snake.	A small, harmless, grayish-colored snake which has a two or three-inch horn on the end of its tail; by some the horn is believed to be deadly poisonous.
Hoop Snake.	A mythical snake that, when frightened, sticks its tail in its mouth, makes a hoop of its body, and rools away in fright.
Indian Hen.	See *Shidepoke.*
Jointed Snake.	A snake that is said to fly to pieces when struck. After sundown, the segments reassemble, knit back together, and the snake in none the worse for having been disjoined.
Josie Goat.	Any Nanny (she-) goat that bears two or more kids at a time.
Joree.	A small bird, probably akin to the grosbears.
July-Fly.	A species of Cicada; also called a locust.
Kildee.	The kildeer plover.
Lord-God.	A very beautiful, large, red-crested climbing bird of the woodpecker family, now almost extinct.
Lungungerer.	Any unusually large fish.

May Colt.   Any horse or mule that, while under saddle or in harness, is predisposed to lie down in water. It is claimed that horses and mules born in the month of May have a penchant for lying down in water while being ridden or driven across a stream. Otherwise, they are not so inclined.

May Pop.   The passion flower, and its fruit.

Mosquito Hawk.   See *Snake Doctor*.

Partridge.   The bob white quail of the South.

Periwinkle.   Locally, erroneously applied by fishermen to the helgramite, etc.

Peckerwood.   A woodpecker.

Quince-edonia.   The quince tree; also its fruit.

Rattan.   A kind of vine-like, creeping plant, altogether foreign to the Rattan of botany.

Razor-back.   A long-snouted, arched-back, piney-wood hog. Any poor hog.

Rain Crow.   A Georgia bird which by emitting a mournful call foretells rain.

Rattlesnake's Pilot.   A female rattlesnake.

Rusticut.   A small, black lizzard.

Scissor-bell.   A goose or gander. (Also, Scissor Bill—a gander, and Scissor Belle—a goose.)

Shirt-tail Johnnie.   A red-headed, white-bodied woodpecker.

Snake Doctor.   The dragon fly.

Scorpion.   Any red-headed lizzard; also any small chameleon.

Stump-sucker.   A horse or mule addicted to the habit of seizing a piece of stationary wood in its mouth, rearing back on its haunches and indulging in a series of nauseating, wheezing groans. Such animals are deemed practically worthless.

Stump-knocker.   The strawberry bass; a small, beautifully colored perch.

Stinking Jim.	A small, cloriferous terrapin, deemed unfit for food.
Sand Sifter.	A brown sand lizzard; a very swift runner.
Stingeree.	The sting ray.
Shidepoke.	A wading bird: The Indian hen or blue heron of several Southern states.
Skippers.	The larvae of certain blow-flies; maggots that get into fresh and cured meats.
Scrooch owl.	A kind of owl that is said to fraternize with its intended prey, gain its confidence, then seize it and devor it at leisure.
Scaly Bark.	The shag-bark hickory; also the nut it bears.
Tacky.	A sorry, undersized, no-account, runty pony.
Thousand Legs.	A centipede.
Vamvamper.	A snapping turtle.
Wolf.	A bot; the larva of the botfly.
Wiggletails.	The larvae of mosquitoes.
War-mouth.	A large-mouthed, game fish of the perch family.
Whipporee.	The whip ray.
Yellow Hammer.	The flicker, or golden-winged woodpecker.

SOURCES

1. Field Worker: Le Garde S. Doughty. Augusta. 1938.
   Field Worker: Louise McKinney. Fannin and Gilmer Counties. June, 1936.
   Field Worker: J. R. Jones. Columbus. 1937.
   Field Worker: M. H. Dauphin. 1937.
2. Informant: Hattie Taylor, ex-slave. Columbus. Field Worker: J. R. Jones. 1936.
   Field Worker: Nan Bagby Stephens.
   Field Worker: Harriett Hattworth.
3. Field Worker: Louise McKinney. Fannin and Gilmer Counties. June 1936.
   Field Worker: Frances Adair.
4. Field Worker: W. W. Linton.
   Field Worker: LeGarde S. Doughty. Augusta.
   Field Worker: J. R. Jones. Columbus. 1937.
5. Field Worker: W. C. Massey. Thomas County. 1937.
   Field Worker: J. R. Jones. Columbus. 1937.

6. This description of a wolf pit is dated June, 1930. A note across the top of the page identifies the writer as George Paulk of Ocilla. It was probably added to the collection by a field worker.
7. Written in 1937 by Field Worker J. R. Jones.

CHAPTER VIII

BELIEFS AND CUSTOMS:
LOVE, MARRIAGE, AND DEATH

New moon, new moon,
Let me see
Who my husband is to be;
The color of his hair,
The clothes he wears,
And the happy day
He is to wed me.[1]

If folk beliefs are true, then every young Georgia woman who recites these lines while looking over her left shoulder at a new moon is certain to find love and marriage. Folklore is filled with similar superstitions, signs, and customs in which verbal charms are used to manipulate the future. They display a belief in the mystical power of words as they relate to the most elemental and important events of every human life: love, marriage, and death.

This collection contains Georgia superstitions and signs pertaining to love and marriage, love potions for ensnaring a loved one, signs which deny someone the joy of matrimony, dreams foretelling a future love, various wedding customs, and death. Some of these beliefs coach a young man in the art of stealing a kiss, while others present the shy with a sure formula for proposing marriage. If a young couple stop on a hill and the moon is full, a young man must kiss her to ensure them both good luck. To see a shooting star while out strolling imposes the same amorous responsibility. If a young man saves a red ear of corn to present to his girl at a corn husking, and she accepts it, they are engaged.

In Georgia's rural society in which the future of nearly every girl was marriage and a family, superstitions concerning love

195

flourished. The unmarried female had to be careful at every minute because she wouldn't find a husband if she sat on a table or took the last piece of bread from a plate. Signs of love were numerous: an untied shoe lace, dropping a dish cloth, or making a unintentional rhyme.

Of the multitude of superstitions gleaned from the collected folklore, however, the largest number concern death. This concern is natural in a society with high infant mortality and few doctors. When a cow lows at night or an owl hoots, it is a signal of approaching death. When a dog crawls on his stomach he is measuring someone's grave. When you shiver with no apparent reason, someone has stepped on your grave.

This concern with death is revealed by the flourishing throughout the last century of the Georgia Negro Burying Society. This society was a kind of cooperative agency in which members, in return for their regular payment of dues, assured themselves a proper funeral. One could have a foretaste of the grandeur of his own burial by attending the laying away of a friend and society member. The brothers and sisters assembled at the home of the deceased; they wore white uniforms with black hats and white cotton gloves. Stretched diagonally across the chests were purple satin bands lettered in white with the name of the society. A group of high dignitaries of the society functioned as honorary pall bearers. These marched or rode in the funeral procession before the hearse. The others marched on foot, a grand turn-out headed by colorful banners. For an extra sum, a brass band would head the procession, stepping briskly along jazzing, "Nearer my God to Thee," "Shall we Gather at the River?" or "When the Saints Go Marching In." The excitement of the occasion did not overshadow the mourning, which was loud and plenteous. Around the grave a quartet sang several selections in rich, natural harmony. The grave was filled and garnished with wax flowers which would later be removed and carried back to the undertaker's to serve at the next burying society funeral.

LOVE POTIONS[1]

If a woman wishes to make a man fall in love with her, she has only to take the small bow usually found in the back of a man's cap on the sweatband, or the bow usually found on the band of the man's hat. After this has been secured it must be taken and worn under her clothes next to her body.

If a man wishes to make a woman fall in love with him all that he has to do is to take some of her hair, tie it up, and then throw it into running water. In a short while she will fall deeply in love with him.

A man may also cause a woman to fall in love with him by letting her drink whiskey in which he has allowed gin-root to soak.

Drop a coin in the spring to bring back a wandering lover. The coin should be rubbed so as to shine through the water.

SIGNS THAT YOU WON'T MARRY[2]

You won't get married if
>   you fall up the steps.
>   any one sweeps beneath your feet.
>   you walk under a ladder.
>   a girl takes the last piece of bread on the plate at meals.
>   you sit on a table.
>   the chair in which your love is sitting falls backward as he or she rises.

A hat put on a bed is the sign that whoever sleeps on that bed will never have a lover.

If the engagement ring is slipped onto the wrong finger, the marriage will never be consummated.

Don't give your sweetheart a knife. It will cut your love in two.

SEEING AND DREAMING
OF ONE'S INTENDED[3]

If you hold a mirror over a well at twelve o'clock on the first day of May, you will see reflected the image of your future husband.

During the first rain in the month of May, run out and look under a large rock. There you will find a hair the color of your future husband's or wife's.

Get a snail on the first day of May and put it on a dish of meal. In crawling the snail will form the initials of your future sweetheart.

Put a handkerchief on a sagebush before the dew falls on the first day of May and your sweetheart's initials will be formed on the handkerchief.

To see the face of her future husband a girl must go alone into a dark room with a lighted candle in her hand on Halloween night. As she faces a mirror she will see the face of the man she will marry peering over her left shoulder.

After paring an apple, in the process of which care is taken to keep the peeling in one piece, throw the skin over the left shoulder. When it lands it will form the initial of the person you are to wed.

Wearing the petticoat wrong side out will cause you to see the man you are to marry before the day is over.

On her birthday a girl may look in a well and see her future husband's face.

SIGNS OF LOVE

If you can blow all the down from a thistle (Shepherd's Clock) with one breath, your sweetheart loves you.

If you starch your sweetheart's handkerchief, he will love you more.

If a girl's shoe comes untied, her sweetheart is thinking about her.

If you are the first person a cat looks at after he has licked himself, you are going to be married.

If you drop your dishcloth, your sweetheart is coming.

If a grasshopper spits on you, you will marry within a year.

If you make a rhyme unintentionally, kiss your hand and you will see your sweetheart before tomorrow night.

Throw a love vine on a bush; if it grows, your sweetheart loves you.

Throw a kiss at a redbird and see your sweetheart tomorrow.

Bend down the leaf of a mullein plant and name it for a person. If it grows back up, the person you named it for loves you.

Turn around on one heel three times and look in the heel print. There you will find a hair the color of your future husband's or wife's hair.

If a girl, sleeping in a strange room for the first time, will name the corners of the room with the names of four young men, the first corner that she sees on awakening will be that with the name of the man she will marry.

Put a piece of wedding cake under your pillow and sleep over it, and whoever you dream about will be your husband or wife.

If you wish the course of true love to run smoothly, walk dowstairs backwards the first morning after you are engaged.

L O V E   V E R S E S[4]

If you wish to dream of your intended, you must put a nightcap under your pillow and say these words on Friday night:

> *This Friday night I go to bed.*
> *I place this night cap under my head,*
> *To dream of the living and not of the dead,*
> *To dream of the one that I should wed.*

If you wish to see your lover, throw salt on the fire five successive mornings and say:

> *It is not salt I mean to burn*
> *But my true love's heart I mean to turn;*
> *Wishing him neither joy nor sleep*
> *'Till he comes back to me!*

This is a popular verse recited often before blowing on the Shepherd's Clock (thistle) to determine if your lover is true:

> *What o'clock, Sweet Margery?'*
> *Said Willie at the gate,*
> *"It's half past kissing-time," she smiled,*
> *"So you are just too late."*
>
> *But taking her small hand in his*
> *and picking up the flower*
> *He showed her how to set it back*
> *exactly half an hour.*
>
> *Sweet Margery at the garden gate*
> *A Shepherd horn she blew;*
> *And "One," she cried, and "Two," she cried*
> *as down the petals flew.*[5]

One should not marry in black, and the following should be observed in choosing a wedding gown:

> *Marry in green, ashamed to be seen.*
> *Marry in brown, a house in town.*

A Man, a Maid, a Moon

Marry in red, wish you were dead.
Marry in yellow, ashamed of the fellow.
Marry in blue, you've chosen true.
Marry in white, and you marry all right.

THE WEDDING[6]

For wedding luck the bride must wear something old and something new, something borrowed, and something blue, and a gold dollar in her shoe.

An old Southern custom says that the bride must not be seen in public between the time the wedding invitations are issued and the ceremony.

The custom of using a ring in the marriage ceremony stems from a belief that the so-called ring finger has a blood vessel which leads to the heart.

It is bad luck for a bride to try on her full bridal array at one time until she dons it for her wedding.

It was once customary for the bride and the groom to jump over a broom together before they were pronounced man and wife.

When the bride throws her bouquet to her unmarried girl friends, the girl who catches it will be the next to marry.

To insure financial success, a bride should have an old coin in her shoe when getting married. The coin should be handed down through the generations to make the charm most effective.

A couple will never prosper until the wedding clothes are worn out.

D E A T H   S I G N S[7]

If a dog cringes from a sick person, it means death is near.

If you point your finger at a grave, you will be the next one to be buried in the cemetery.

If a mourning dove or an owl flies into the bedroom of a sick person, the life span of that person will be very, very short.

Expect death if a red bird pecks on the window.

Expect death if a strange dog comes and howls by your home.

A picture falling from the wall signifies death.

To stir cream into milk with a fork will cause serious trouble, even death itself, to come to your home.

If a chicken crows after it goes to roost, it must be killed that night or some member of the family will die.

To carry a garden tool through the house causes the early death of a member of the household.

If a screech owl cries, take off your shoes and turn them over; then you will escape death and the screech owl will stop his cries.

If you plant a cypress vine on your house, some members of the family will die.

If a measuring worm gets on you it is measuring you for new garments; some say for your coffin.

To sneeze at the breakfast table is a sign that a friend shall die within three days.

If you sweep under a sickbed the patient will die.

If one dreams of his teeth falling out, some member of his family will soon die.

Never skip a row in planting cotton. For every row not planted there will be a death in the family or among its relations that year.

Walking under a ladder forebodes an untimely death.

To sneeze with a mouth full of food is an indication of impending death.

For a horse to strike sparks denotes the death of someone in the household.

If you kill a frog, someone in the family will die.

A whippoorwill's or an owl's singing near a house means a death in the family.

A ringing in the ears is a death knell for someone who is dying or will die very soon.

If you see three white horses at once, they signify death.

If clothes are washed on New Year's Day, the one who washes them will wash for a corpse before the year is over.

When a cow lows at night, it signals death.

The soul of a person who dies singing is going to heaven.

If two people are sick in the same bed, one will die from the disease with which he is afflicted and the other will live.

Do not say a casket is pretty or you will soon be in one yourself.

If one is buried in a lone grave by a stream, the stream will catch the spirit on its way to God; and when the moon is new, the singing of the deceased can be heard above the music of the water.

The first person buried in a new graveyard will never "lie sweet" but will always be a restless spirit.

If a body does not stiffen soon after death, some other member of the family will soon follow.

If a ring is dropped during the wedding ceremony, the bride will soon die.

Do not sweep the floor of a house you are moving into, nor sweep the trash out of the door; it is a sign some member of the family will be carried out before twelve months have passed.

When a dog crawls on his stomach he is measuring someone's grave.

If a dog refuses to eat food from the plate of a sick person, it signifies that person will soon die.

Never measure the dead for apparel or a casket, for this will result in a restless spirit.

To change the position of a sick person's bed means the person will die soon.

If a rooster comes to the house, turns his head towards the door and crows, it signifies the death of a relative.

Do not meet a funeral procession, for it portends that you will lose one of your relatives.

If a grave is dug the day before a burial another death will occur within seven days.

To sew for a person who is sick is to put stitches in his shroud.

If a person who is ill picks at the covers, it portends death.

If you suddenly shiver, a rabbit is running across your grave.

If a chair rocks after you get up from it, death sits in it and marks you for himself. Sit quickly and cross your fingers three times to protect yourself.

If an ominous black cloud gathers while a person lies dying, it signifies God's disapproval and means the one dying is sure to go to Hell.

If two persons part company at a fence, they will soon be separated by death.

Death will result if the wood of the sassafras is burned.

If a woman cuts out a dress on Friday, she will die before it is worn out.

If a man's nose bleeds after he is dead, it is a sign he has been killed.

If you count the cars in a funeral procession there will be another funeral in the number of days that there are cars.

When the hands of a dead person remain limp, some other member of the family will soon follow him in death.

If a buzzard lights on top of the house, there is to be a death within.

Trunks and tables are close kin to coffins and cooling boards. Never sit on them, for mortal ailments will follow.

If you see your own face reflected in the glass of a hearse, you will be the next corpse.

If you wear anything new to a funeral, you will hear of a death in your family.

If you count the cars at a funeral, the next death will be in your home.

It is considered fatal to be the first person who crosses a new bridge.

DEATH CUSTOMS AND BELIEFS[8]

A mirror is placed over the mouth to detect death. If no moisture gathers, the person is dead. If a pin stuck into the flesh leaves a hole, the person is dead; if alive, the hole will close and blood will appear.

If there is a frown on the face of a dying person, he is a sinner; and if there is a smile on his face, he is a Christian.

A body must never be allowed to be in a room alone after it has been prepared for burial. Friends must sit up with the corpse.

A saucer of salt is placed on the chest of a corpse to prevent purging.

The dead should not be buried for three days. A relative or friend must remain with the corpse, so that when the soul comes back to view the body, it will not feel lonesome.

Face a coffin by sitting at a table with a breeze on your back.

It is always considered as bad luck to sweep or to clean a house before the body is buried.

When the deceased is buried, his feet should face the east and his head should face the west. According to some, the person is then "straight with the world."

The bed of a person who is dying hard should be moved so as to face east and west, and his death will be made easier.

The dead should always be buried with their faces toward the east and then they will comply with the old saying: "When the resurrection comes . . ."

If a clock is not covered in the house where a death occurs, it will never run again.

If the pictures in a house are not turned toward the wall after a death, some other member of the family will die.

If you put your hand on the head of a dead man, you will never worry about him, he will never haunt you, and you will never fear death.

Beds are seldom taken down immediately after the person expires, else you will have another death in the family.

When a rural person dies his family and friends hold "settin' ups." These are not necessarily solem vigils over the dead but the friendly visits of long-separated neighbors. Refreshments are generally served during the night and much morbid enjoyment is found in comparing accounts of sickness and death. To talk of anything else is not considered proper.

Formerly a house of mourning was closed to all entertainment for two years, and its feminine occupants had to creep about like ghosts or hermits because it was scandalous to be seen in public unless pottering around in a cemetery.

The custom of wearing mourning consisted of a widow unfailingly draping herself in "weeds" for two years; lightening to second mourning, meaning with the veil off the face and with touches of white at throat and wrists, for one year more; followed by a six months' emergence from weeds into violet before the widow could be said to be "out of mourning."

Men normally wore arm bands of crepe for six months. Some Negroes wore crepe hearts sewn on the sleeve. A certain not overly-grieved widow, while obeying the dictates of mourning apparel outwardly, relieved her taste for colors by wearing bright red night gowns and undergarments.

If a piece of the dead man's hair is put in a certain spot, you will always know where his spirit is; and if you remove the hair, you will be haunted.

Never cross or pass a funeral procession, or you will be the next one to die.

When a person has drowned in deep water, throw in a bundle of fodder and it will float around and around until it "smells death," and then come to a halt above the dead.

The dead come back and call for the living. A violent death leaves the soul without a resting place and causes it to roam the earth.

A branch of a thorn bush hung on the head of a bed of illness wards off death as long as the thorns are sharp.

If you see a dead man in the mirror, you will be unlucky the rest of your life.

Be sure to throw away the comb and brush of a dead person, for it would be bad luck for anybody to use it.

Burn the clothing of the dead and any clothes that have a bad odor or in which a person has died, for they are poisonous.

BURIAL CUSTOMS

To make a grave "sweet" the rays of the setting sun must fall on it and then it must be filled as night falls, often by the light of pine knot torches.

A grave should be decorated with the possessions of the departed one so that the soul may rest in peace.

In Savannah and other coastal towns, the graves in some Negro cemeteries are covered with broken bits of blue china and glass, blue plates and vases, and all sorts of charms to ward off evil spirits.

Many personal articles of the deceased—a child's favorite toy, etc.—are frequently placed on the grave. One grave in a country cemetery was seen decorated with all the medicine bottles and pill boxes used in the last illness of the dead person.

Stones are not normally thrown on graves in Georgia, but in many instances a light is left burning on a grave for a certain length of time for the purpose of lighting the way of the newly dead through the shadows of the spirit world.

The walking stick of an old man or the crutch of a cripple must always be laid on the grave, lest the soul be retarded in flight.

If you plant a cedar tree you will die when it grows large enough to shade your grave.

SOURCES

1. Field Worker: Martha G. Bell. 1936.
2. Field Worker: Grace McCune. Athens. February. 1939.
3. Field Worker: Maude Barragan. Augusta.
4. Field Worker: Martha G. Bell.
5. Field Worker: Nan Bagby Stephens. 1937.

6. Informant: Harry Raynes, Augusta. Field Worker: Edith Bell Love. 1938.
   Field Worker: LeGarde S. Douthty.
7. Informant: Mrs. Ellen Lindsay. Atlanta. Field Worker: Minnie B. Ross. 1937.
   Field Worker: Mary Johnson. Macon.
   Field Worker: Martha G. Bell.
8. Informant: Rebecca Conn. Washington. Field Worker: Mrs. Rebecca Stonestreet. 1938.
   Field Worker: Edith Bell Love.

CHAPTER IX

CHILDREN'S LORE

Like children everywhere, the Georgia child grew into adulthood inescapably passing through various stages of association with the oral tradition. The lullabye sung by his mother was seldom learned from a book. Crooning, chanting, and numbers games like "Eeny, Meenie, Minie, Moe" were derived from the traditions of the parents. Since children are the most conservative group in any society, few new games or songs are added to children's folklore in any one generation. Those that enter the tradition usually last for centuries. The Georgia child experienced a unique influence in the person of his Negro Mammy, who brought with her children's lore, superstitions, and home medical cures to protect the child.

The mysteries of sex were explained to children with far-fetched tales. Since most babies were born at home, the curious older brother or sister was told that the new baby "came out of a hollow log," "was found in an old stump," "was laid in a watermelon patch," or "was brought by the doctor in his black satchel."[1]

Folklore concerning the child in his natal period is extensive. Folk belief assumes that if the mother is frightened, the child can be marked by the trauma. One pregnant woman saw her husband bleeding a mule, and the child was marked with a blood-red birthmark. The baby who slithered like a snake was believed to have been so affected when the mother inadvertently caught some boys killing a rattler. The pregnant woman's diet had to be carefully controlled, too, because eating twin apples or other fruit would cause her to bear twins.

The child demanded almost constant care from the day of its birth. The mother or nurse watched that no one cut the hair of an infant before it was a year old or it would become weak-backed and die. No one was allowed to step over a child because to do so would stop its growth. To sweep under a girl child's feet doomed her to spinsterhood. An extensive lore of folk medicine both protected and cured the infant. To prevent the usual stomach trouble during teething, one had the baby gaze in a hand mirror before it was four weeks old. To cure it of sore throat, the baby was given seven sips of water from the nearest brook.

The folklore of children themselves reaches from "This little piggy went to market" to songs, riddles, and games. The child often learns to count by means of a traditional song, and he probably encounters sexual love and a childish kiss for the first time in a folk game. One of the most important and extensive influences on the growing child remains the vast body of traditional folklore through which he passes as he grows to adulthood.

C H I L D C A R E[2]

A child born during the summer months will perspire freely.

Children born with cauls possess the power to see ghosts and have other superhuman attributes.

If a baby is born with caul on its face, it will never drown in the sea.

Don't drink water out of a bucket carried on a child's head; to do so will stop the child's growth.

Tying the toe nail of a quail to a baby's ankle will make it quick on its feet.

If you step over a reclining child you will stop its growth.

If you measure an infant it will die before it is grown.

To spare a child sickness caused by growing too fast, four grown people who love it must stand in the four corners of the room in which it was born and throw it from corner to corner to corner and then diagonally to form the pattern of a cross.

Tickling a young child causes it to stutter.

The fingernails of a young baby must be bitten; if you cut them, you will make a thief of him.

If you cut off a baby's fingernails, it will die before it is six months old.

A child's disposition will be patterned after that of the person who first takes it out-of-doors.

When a new baby has a spasm, pull its clothes off and throw them in the fire. It will not have another.

Mountain people lift the fallen palate in the mouth of a child by seating him in a chair; then they lift him chair and all by the hair of the head.

To make a baby walk early, he should be made to stand behind a door and be stroked downward with a broom. This should be repeated every day for one week.

Rub greasy dish water on children's knees and they will walk early.

To cure a child of sore mouth, give it seven sips of water from the nearest brook.

When a baby has thrash (sore mouth), brew tea of nine saw bugs and make him drink it; if this fails to cure, send for an old woman who will cross two sticks in his mouth while talking in an unknown tongue.

Putting a hat on a baby's head will cause bad teething, as will letting it look into a mirror.

Before a baby reaches the age of four weeks allow him to gaze into a hand mirror. The reflection causes the baby to acquire teeth without the usual stomach troubles.

Put a string of dog's teeth around the neck of a teething infant to encourage the child's teeth to come through.

Tie nine small buttons on a string around a baby's neck to make it teethe easily.

Mullein tea is prescribed for teething babies.

If a baby teethes early, it is making way for a new baby.

A mole's foot tied in a cloth and hung around a baby's neck will make teething easy.

To make teething easy for a baby, its gums should be massaged with the raw brains of a rabbit.

The tip of a buzzard's claw worn in a bag about the neck makes teething easy.

A bag of allspice worn around the neck of the baby facilitates the cutting of teeth.

To let a puppy eat with a baby and lick its face prevents illness.

Let a new-born baby suck a piece of fat meat and it will always be healthy.

A tea made of button bush berries acts as a tonic for children.

The most widely used preventive medicine for children is asafetida. A small bag with asafetida is usually worn around the neck. This protective medicine has a very peculiar odor and is considered offensive by most people. The following folk story adequately describes asafetida's potent smell.

"Once there was a woman who sent her husband to a drug store to get some asafetida, and on the way back he was caught in a heavy rain and the asafetida was soaked, which increased the offensive odor. When he got home, his little boy climbed onto his lap and was playing with him when he suddenly exclaimed, 'Ma, Pa is dead and don't know it.' "[3]

DISCIPLINE FOR CHILDREN[4]

Disciplining of children once consisted mostly of threats and of tales of strange people or creatures who would mete out punishment. The threat most frequently made was that "a booger man will get you." This strange creature was never defined or described. Other common threats included: "The garbage man will get you if you ain't good;" "The big black dog will get you;" "The soap woman will boil you and make you into a bar of soap." Old crones usually played with the children's nurse, asking, "Is this child good?" And the child was no doubt relieved to hear the nurse reply, "Yessum, he's good." In Rome, Georgia, children were threatened that Uncle Lewis would get them and put them in the bag slung over his shoulder if they misbehaved. Variations were added to the familiar arguments for inducing good behavior at Christmas time. Children were not only told that Santa Claus came only to good boys and girls, but they were warned that Santa would throw hot ashes in the faces of children who didn't go to sleep. Children who weren't good would receive hickory sticks instead of toys. The most practical disciplinary measure was the peach tree switch. Children were informed that the peach tree grew long switches for the express purpose of tanning little boys' bottoms.

ENTERTAINMENT

The children of past years created their own entertainment with a vast children's lore. They laughed at their own riddles, sang and danced to songs, and the older children played kissing games.

Children's Riddles[5]

1. *"What is round as a bisquit, busy as a bee,*
   You can guess every riddle, but you can't guess me."
   Answer: "A watch."

2. *"Why does a chimney smoke?*
   Answer: "Because it can't chew."

3. *"A riddle, a riddle, as I suppose.*
   A hundred eyes and never a nose. What am I?"
   Answer: "A sifter."

4. *"It can run and can't walk.*
   It has a tongue and can't talk."
   Answer: "A wagon."

5. *"Hippy, tippy, up stairs,*
   Hippy, tippy, down stairs,
   If you go near hippy tippy, he'll bite you."
   Answer: "A hornet."

6. *"East and west and north and south*
   Ten thousand teeth and never a mouth."
   Answer: "A device for carding wool."

7. *"What do you have that everybody else uses more*
   than you do?"
   Answer: "Your name."

CHILDREN'S SONGS AND GAMES

The children's songs often helped them to go to sleep, to learn to count, or to recite the alphabet. Folklorists have identified more than four hundred rhymes for these purposes. Many of the folk songs of Georgia were familiar English ballads which had changed through constant local use. One of the most popular types of songs was used for counting out for various games. Usually there were a greater number of words in the rhyme than there were children in the group. Having completed the verse or sentence, the child to whom the last word was said, was "out," and stepped aside. A common ending of the counting out songs was "one, two, three, out goes she (or he)!"

One-ery[6]
(Counting out song)

One-ery, two-ery, ickery, Ann.
Fillicy, fallacy, Nicholas, John,
Queever, quaver, English knaver,
Stickelum, stanckelum, Jericho, buck!

William-a[7]
(Counting out song)

William-a, William-a trimble toe,
He's a good fisherman,
Catches hens, puts 'em in pens,
Some lay eggs and some lay none.

Wire, brier (pronounced wi-yer, bri-yer) limber, lock,
Three wild geese in a flock,
One flew east,
One flew west,
One flew over the cuckoo's nest.

O-U-T Spells OUT GOES SHE
Down to the bottom of the deep, blue sea.

Old Dan Tucker[8]

Old Dan Tucker was a fine ole man,
He washed his face in a fryin' pan;
Combed his hair with a wagon wheel,
Died with a toothache in his heel.

Old Dan tucker, he got drunk,
Fell in the fire, kicked up a chunk;
Red hot coals in his shoe,
Laws a-mussy, how de ashes flew."

My Pretty Little Pink[9]
(Game Song)

Here is a game and song used by the children of the mountains. One girl who is called "the pretty little pink" stands in the center of the circle while the others march around her singing.

My pretty little pink, I once did think
That you and I would marry,
But now I've lost all hopes of that,
I can no longer tarry.
I've got my knapsack on my back,
My musket on my shoulder,
To march away to Mexico,
To be a gallant soldier.
Where coffee grows on the white oak tree
And the rivers flow with brandy,
Where the boys are like a lump of gold,
And the girls as sweet as candy.

This Lady Wears a Dark Green Shawl
(Game Song)

Two children in the center of the ring carry on the action.

They choose others as the game goes on. When there is no one
left to sing the game is over.

> *This lady she wears a dark-green-shawl,*
> *A dark-green-shawl, a dark-green-shawl,*
> *This lady she wears a dark-green-shawl,*
> *I love her to my heart!*
> *Now choose for your lover, honey, my love!*
>
> *Honey, my love! honey, my love!*
> *Now choose for your lover,*
> *Honey, my love!*
> *I love her to my heart!*
> *Now dance with your lover, honey my love,*
> *Throw your arms round your lover!*
> *Farewell to your lover!*

Marching 'Round the Level
(Game Song)

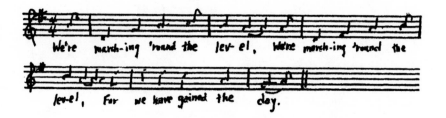

A group of children join hands and form a circle, marching
around, one child in center of ring. All of the children then
sing:

> *We're marching 'round the level*
> *(repeat three times)*
> *For we have gained the day.*

Happy Games of Childhood

The marching stops and the child in the center stands before his or her favorite, while they all continue to sing:

> *One kiss before I leave you*
> *(repeat three times)*
> *For we have gained the day.*

As this verse is sung, the child in the circle chases his favorite before whom he has stood and if caught has the privilege of kissing her or him. The game is continued in this manner and the one caught is placed in the center of the circle.

One Sort, Two Sort
(Drawl Song)

The drawl song merges some of the Indian alphabet with the Latin of the Roman Catholic chants and the grit of the rural vernacular. Boys and girls line up on opposite sides of a straight line, one being left to count in a slow, lazy tone. He begins at one end of the line and drawls the following:

> *One sort, two sort, three sort, sand*
> *Bob tail Dominie little taw tan,*
> *Virgin Mary, halem, caelem, siglam, zaglam, BUCK!*

He counts one person on each beat or accent and the person that the word *Buck* comes out on, rushes to catch the others as they immediately scatter to one side of the line and when they attempt to cross the line they may be caught, at which point the caught child becomes "It" and chases the others.

Little Sallie Saucer
(Game Song)

In this game song one child is left inside the ring. As the circle is formed around her, she sits down and puts her hands over her eyes and feigns weeping. Children in the circle march around and sing:

Little Sallie Saucer
Sitting in the water,
Crying and a-weeping
For what she has done.

Sallie rises and wipes her eyes, as children continue to sing:

Oh, rise, Sallie, rise
And wipe your weeping eyes,
Turn to the east
And turn to the west
And turn to the one you love best.

Sallie chooses the one she loves best, who goes into the ring and becomes Sallie, while the other child takes her place in the circle, as the song continues.

High O
(Game Song)

In "High O" swift action takes place. Some child skips quickly around inside of the ring, then chooses another, and takes her place.

In come another one, High O!
A mighty pretty little one,
High O!
Then get about, go!
High O!
Then get about go!
High O!

What Time, Old Witch
(Game Song)

Fourteen children usually play the game, one for the witch, one for the mother, and twelve for her children, who represent the twelve hours of daylight.

The witch stands a few feet away from the mother and her

twelve children. The mother leaves her group, presumably to go to the well to drink and wash her feet. While she is away the old witch comes and steals one of the children. Upon the mother's return, she and her remaining children go in a body to visit the witch and sing together these words:

> *I went to the well to wash my toe,*
> *When I got back my chicken was gone.*
> *What time old witch?*
> *Chicken, chicken, crane or crow? (Repeat)*

The witch replies, "One!" and makes a grab for another child, who is protected by the mother and other children, who begin to run home. If the witch is successful there will be two children with her. The game is then repeated from the beginning. This time the witch will reply, "Two!" as she has two of the children caught, and so on, until all twelve are captured. At the end of the game the children choose a new mother and a new witch and then repeat the same routine.

The May Pole Song[10]
(Game Song)

This is a game played primarily by girls. The children form a ring and sing the following words as one girl skips about inside the ring.

> *All around the May pole, the May pole, the May pole,*
> *All around the May pole, now Miss Sallie won't you bow?*
> *Now Miss Sallie, won't you bow?*
> *Now Miss Sallie, won't you jump for joy, jump for*
> *joy, jump for joy*
> *Now Miss Sallie, won't you jump for joy?*
> *Now Miss Sallie, won't you bow?*

At the beginning of the second line, the girl bows to the one she chooses. Then both "jump for joy." A peculiar step, somewhat like a clog, not at all easy to imitate, is taken. The game song is begun again and a second girl skips about the ring.

Sapsucker[11]

See that sapsucker on that pine!
Oh, how I wish that girl was mine.
I got drunk and away she fled—
Ever since that my head's been red

High the raccoon climbed the pine,
His feet all gummed in turpentine;
Old belled cow run down the lane,
Bone in her mouth and couldn't chew her grain.

Set my hen in a fodder stack;
Come along a hawk and hit 'er in the back.
She flew off in a cack, cack, cack,
And her old bones went whickety whack!

Take your Lover in the Ring

"Take your Lover in the Ring" is a Georgia folksong sung primarily by children and dating from slavery times. The children's action during the singing probably matched the words of the song.

My old mistress promised me.
Before she died she'd set me free.

Take your lover in the ring. I don't care!
Take your lover in the ring. I don't care!

Now she's dead and gone to hell.
I hope that the devil will burn her well!

Take your lover in the ring. I don't care!
Take your lover in the ring. I don't care!

I wouldn't be a Rebel to tote a Rebel's gun,
I would rather be a Yankee to see the Rebels run.

It's a golden ring. I don't care!
It's a golden ring. I don't care!

I've Been to See Miss Jenny-Mae-Jo

Each stanza is sung by a different person. The whole group answers the question and then another singer takes over.

> *I've been to see Miss Jenny-Mae-Jo,*
> *Miss Jenny-Mae-Jo, Miss Jenny-Mae-Jo,*
> *I've been to see Miss Jenny-Mae-Jo,*
> *And how is she today?*

Answers:

> *She's washing'.*
> *She's rich.*
> *She's hanging out clothes.*
> *She's ironin'.*
> *She's better.*
> *She's worse.*
> *She's dead.*

Children's Quatrains

> *De racoon's tail am bushy,*
> *De possum's tail am bare,*
> *De rabbit got no tail at all,*
> *Jes' a little bunch o' hair.*

> *Chicken in de' bread tray,*
> *Scratchin' at de dough,*
> *Granny, will yo' dog bite?*
> *No, chile, no.*

> *One ole man come ridin' by.*
> *Says I, 'Ole man, yo' horse gwine die.'*
> *Ef he die, I'll tan his skin.*
> *Ef he live, I'll ride him 'gin.*

Many, Many Stars[12]
(Kissing Song)

The ring games and songs of early childhood soon gave way to kissing games when the young people reached the age of twelve. Practically all of these are played by selecting someone to be "it" who stands in the middle of a circle of players who then join hands and march around singing, at the close of which the person kisses someone who then takes his place and the game goes on.

> *Many, many stars are in the sky,*
> *Some as old as Adam,*
> *Down upon your knees and kiss who you please,*
> *Your humble servant, Madam.*

The person in the center goes down upon one knee before the girl of his selection and she kisses him.

Higher Up the Cherry Tree
(Kissing Song)

> *Higher up the cherry tree*
> *Riper grow the berries*
> *Soon a young man courts a girl,*
> *Sooner they will marry.*
>
> *Courts a girl with sky-blue eyes*
> *Courts a girl with money,*
> *Courts a girl with sunny smiles,*
> *Kiss her and call her 'honey!'*

Old Green Field[13]

A leader and a ring of young people sing alternately the following lyrics.

Old green field, Rock to your love!
Old green field, Rock to your love!
Tell me who you love! Rock to your love!
O Miss _____ (You call a name)
Come take a set right beside your love!
Kiss her once and let her go.
Don't let her sit in this chair no mo'
Old green field, Rock to your love!
Old green field, Rock to your love!

SOURCES

1. Field Worker: J. R. Jones. Columbus. 1937. Note reads "From personal knowledge."
2. Informant: Julia Henderson, ex-slave. Augusta. Field Worker: Maude Barragan. June. 1939.
   Informant: Carrie Nancy Fryer. Child Nursemaid. Augusta. Field Worker: Maude Barragan. Nov., 1937.
3. Field Worker: Nancy Bagby Stephens.
4. Informant: Negro nursemaid in Columbus. Field Worker: J. R. Jones. 1937.
5. Field Worker: Harriett Hallworth.
6. Field Worker: Harriett Hallworth.
7. Field Worker: Edith Bell Love. Augusta.
8. Field Worker: Harriett Hallworth.
9. Field Worker: Edith Bell Love. Augusta.
10. Field Worker: Harriett Hallworth.
11. Field Worker: George Ward. 1937.
12. Field Worker: Edith Bell Love. Augusta.
13. Field Worker: William Kermit.

CHAPTER X

F O L K S O N G S

Whenever Georgians have cleared land, felled trees, fought wars, picked cotton, or raised barns, they have done it to the accompaniment of songs—those inherited from their past and those they created from their own experience. Those songs, whether spirituals, traditional ballads, work songs, or nonsense ditties, comment on the changing culture of Georgia and Georgians for over three centuries. Their transmission is traceable largely to numerous waves of immigration into and around the state, first from literally every country in Europe, then from Africa, and finally the steady but considerable influx from the Virginias and the Carolinas.

The folk songs collected here reveal the variety of the state's history. English and Scottish ballads with their variations and corruptions show the prevalence of British settlers. *Lord Randall* in its Georgia version tells the sketchy story of a lover poisoned with Georgia conjure materials like red head and speckle back. *Giles Collins* has been transformed into simply *George Giles*, and *The Jew's Daughter* interestingly has become *The Jeweler's Daughter*. The traditional ballad plots remain the same, however, even after a long period of Georgia domestication.

The work songs included here provide a commentary both on slavery and on the important days of the railroad and turpentine work gangs after the Civil War. Whether in the field or woods or working the rails, a song leader made the group work fast or slow according to the tempo of his singing. A good song leader was therefore always in demand, and the rail bosses paid him a few pennies more, not for his work but for his talent.

The spiritual is one of America's most characteristic art forms, intended originally to express emotional religion. The evangelistic preaching so closely allied with these songs can be traced in Georgia to such early American salvation preachers as Lorenzo Dow and George Whitefield. Since religion centered on Biblical truth these songs, too, borrow both their diction (phrases like "the old ship of Zion" and "Jordon River is chilly and cold") and their subject ("Little Moses") from the Good Book. Often their most touching element lies in the intense concentration on the crucifixion of Christ ("Were You There When They Crucified My Lord?").

Some of the songs collected are of indigenous origin. The tragic death of Marietta's little Mary Phagan is given, and *Frank Dupree* recounts the robbery by and subsequent sentencing of an Atlanta criminal. Some of the plantation songs may very well have seen their birth in the Georgia sun.

Even in so short a collection one fact stands out: the good song, whether drawn from the genius of an artist or from folk traditions, is but a reflection of man's basic experience.

I. WORK SONGS

CHURNING SONG
(Plantation Song for Churning Butter)

> *Come, butter, come.*
> *Peter at de gate.*
> *With a hot johnnycake,*
> *Come butter, come butter,*
> *Come butter, come.*

AXE TALKIN'
(Antiphonal Singing)

Negroes cutting wood in the forest divide themselves into two groups. With axes readied, or thrown up, the first group sings, "Axe talkin'," and as the axes come down exactly at the same time and cut the wood with one sound, the second group sings, "Nobody a-cuttin'," and this is repeated. The first group

Farewell, Sweet Mollie, Adieu!

Steal Miss Liza, Miss Liza Jane.
Steal Miss Liza, Miss Liza Jane.
She lib so long, she got bald
and decided not to die at all,
Miss Liza Jane.

Steal Miss Liza, Miss Liza Jane.
Steal Miss Liza, Miss Liza Jane.

AIN'T I LIVING EASY?

Oh, I got a gal in de white folks' yard;
She steals me meat, she steal me lard;
Oh, every night about half past eight
I hangs my bucket on de white folks' gate.
Oh, ain't I living easy?
Oh, ain't I living easy?

OLD GRUMBLER

Old Grumbler is dead and laid in his grave,
Um, um, laid in his grave.
An apple tree grew right over his head,
Um, um, over his head.

The apples grew ripe and started to drop,
Um, um gather them up.
An old woman came to gather them up,
Um, um, gather them up.
Up rose old Grumbler and hit her ker-pop,
Um, um, hit her ker-pop.

FAREWELL SWEET MOLLIE[3]
(Plantation Song)

There was a young girl who had several sweethearts. She

finally married an old man, and the rejected suitors composed
this song and sang it at her window the night after the marriage:

> *Farewell, sweet Mollie*
> *I bid you adieu;*
> *I am ruined for a-loving you.*
> *I eat when I'm hungry;*
> *I drink when I'm dry,*
> *And think on sweet Mollie,*
> *And sit down and cry.*

GOOD TIME IN GEORGIA

Dere ain't no good times in Georgia,
Like I used to have.
Dere ain't no good times in Georgia,
Like I used to have.
I'm going back to Alabama and git my good gal back.

III. SPIRITUALS AND HYMNS

EVIL LITTLE DAVID[4]

Evil little David, O yes.
Evil little David, O yes.
Evil little David killed Goliath.
Want to get to heaven in the morning.

Evil Little David

I'M GOIN' TO SEE MY JESUS SOON[6]

What a wonder in the moon,
What a wonder in the moon,
What a wonder in the moon,
I'm goin' to see my Jesus soon.

If you don' b'liev' I've been redeemed,
If you don' b'liev' I've been redemmed,
If you don' b'liev' I've been redemmed,
Then follow me down to Jordan's stream.

Jordan's stream so chilly and cold,
Jordan's stream so chilly and cold,
Jordan's stream so chilly and cold,
I got Jesus in my soul.

Two big horses side by side,
Two big horses side by side,
Two big horses side by side,
Me and my Jesus goin' to take a ride.

I'LL SOON BE DONE WITH THE TROUBLES OF THE WORLD

I'll soon be done with the troubles of the world;
Gwine home to live with the Lord.
O, where is my old mother?
O, where is my old mother?
O, where is my old mother?
She's gone home to live with the Lord;
She's gone home to live with the Lord.

I'll soon be done with the troubles of the world;
Gwine home to live with the Lord.
O, where is my old father?
O, where is my old father?
O, where is my old father?
He's gone home to live with the Lord.

I'll soon be done with the troubles of the world.
I'll soon be done with the troubles of the world.
I'll soon be done with the troubles of the world.
Gwine home, gwine home, gwine home,
Gwine home to live with the Lord.

TRYIN' TO MAKE A HUNDRED

I'm singin' tryin' to make a hundred.
I'm singin' tryin' to make a hundred.
Ninety-nine and one-half won't do.
I'm singin' tryin' to make a hundred.
Ninety-nine and a half won't do.

I'm mournin' tryin' to make a hundred.
I'm mournin' tryin' to make a hundred.
Ninety-nine and one-half won't do.
I'm mournin' tryin' to make a hundred.
Ninety-nine and a half won't do.

I'm prayin' tryin' to make a hundred.
I'm prayin' tryin' to make a hundred.
Ninety-nine and one-half won't do.
I'm prayin' to make a hundred.
Ninety-nine and a half won't do.

JUST GOT OVER

Lord, I just got over,
Lord, I just got over,
Lord, I just got over,
Just got over in de Heavenly land.

Old satan mad and I am glad.
Just got over in de Heavenly land.
He missed dat soul he thought he had.
Just got over in de Heavenly land.

Lord, I just got over,
Lord, I just got over,
Lord, I just got over,
Just got over in de Heavenly land.

Mind, my sister, how you walk on de cross.
Your foot might slip and your soul get lost.
Just got over in de Heavenly land.

Lord, I just got over,
Lord, I just got over,
Lord, I just got over,
Just got over in de Heavenly land.

I SHALL NOT BE MOVED

I shall not, I shall not be moved.
I shall not, I shall not be moved.
Just like a tree planted by the waters,
I shall not be moved.

I'm on my way to heav'n, I shall not be moved.
I'm on my way to heav'n, I shall not be moved.
Just like a tree planted by the waters,
I shall not be moved.

King Jesus is my Captain, I shall not be moved.
King Jesus is my Captain, I shall not be moved.
Just like a tree planted by the waters,
I shall not be moved.

OLD SHIP OF ZION

The old ship of Zion,
When she come, when she come.
The old ship of Zion
When she come.

She carried many thousands,
When she come, when she come.
She carried many thousands
When she come.

She carried my mother,
When she come, when she come.
She carried my mother
When she come.

She carried my father,
When she come, when she come.
She carried my father
When she come.

She reeled and she rocked,
When she come, when she come.
She reeled and she rocked
When she come.

She's heavy loaded,
When she come, when she come.
Headed for de ocean
When she come.

The old ship of Zion,
When she come, when she come.
The old ship of Zion
When she come.

WHAT YOU DOIN' IN HERE?

What you doin' in here, ain't got no garments on?
What you doin' in here, ain't got no garments on?
What you doin' in here, ain't got no garments on?
Don't you know God's got his eyes on you?

Some people moaning in the church, ain't got no garments on.
Some people moaning in the church, ain't got no garments on.

Some people moaning in the church, ain't got no garments on.
Don't you know God's got his eyes on you?

Some people prayin' in de church, ain't got no garments on.
Some people prayin' in de church, ain't got no garments on.
Some people prayin' in de church, ain't got no garments on.
Don't you know God's got his eyes on you?

Some people shoutin' in the church, ain't got no garments on.
Some people shoutin' in the church, ain't got no garments on.
Some people shoutin' in the church, ain't got no garments on.
Don't you know God's got his eyes on you?

WHERE DE SUN DON'T NEBER GO DOWN

Where de sun don't neber go down,
Where de sun don't neber go down,
Where de sun don't neber go down,
I promise my Lawd I'd meet him dere.
Where de sun don't neber go down.

Dat's de reason I pray so hard,
Dat's de reason I pray so hard,
Dat's de reason I pray so hard,
'Cause I promise my Lawd I'd meet him dere
Where de sun don't neber go down.

Where de sun don't neber go down,
Where de sun don't neber go down,
Where de sun don't neber go down,
I promise my Lawd I'd meet him dere,
Where de sun don't neber go down.

Dat's de reason I mourned so hard,
Dat's de reason I mourned so hard,
Dat's de reason I mourned so hard,
'Cause I promised my Lawd I'd meet him dere.
Where de sun don't neber go down.

Where de sun don't neber go down,
Where de sun don't neber go down,
Where de sun don't neber go down,
I promised my Lawd I'd meet him dere.
Where de sun don't neber go down.

Dat's de reason I work so hard,
Dat's de reason I work so hard,
Dat's de reason I work so hard,
'Cause I promised my Lawd I'd meet him dere.
Where de sun don't neber go down.

STAY IN DAT FIELD

Stay in dat field, stay in dat field,
Stay in dat field, til de war is ended.
Missionary Baptist is my name, til de war is ended;
Hope I live and die the same, til de war is ended.
Jordan Ribber is chilly and cold, til de war is ended;
Upon de cross I'll never git loss, till de war is ended.
Stay in dat field, stay in dat field,
Stay in dat field, til de war is ended.
If you get to heaven before I do, til the war is ended,
Look out for me, I'm on my way too, til de war is ended.
One day, one day I was walking along, til the war is ended.
I heard a little voice, but I saw no man, til the war is ended.
Said your sins are forgiven and your soul set free, til the war is ended.

I HAVE A LOVING SISTER[8]

I have a loving sister to be bap-per-tized.
I have a loving sister to be bap-per-tized.
I have a loving sister to be bap-per-tized,
Who loves a dying lamb.

Move along, move along; God give you wings to move along.

BLOW, GABRIEL, BLOW

Blow, Gabriel, blow—blow the righteous home!
I belong to the band, halleluyah!
  Halleluyah! Halleluyah!
I do belong to the band, halleluyah!
Blow, Gabriel, blow—blow the righteous home!

If my mother wants to go,
Why don't you come along?
I do belong to the band, halleluyah!
  Halleluyah! Halleluyah!
Blow, Gabriel, blow—blow the righteous home!

If my sister wants to go,
Why don't you come along?
I do belong to the band, halleluyah!
  Halleluyah! Halleluyah!
Blow, Gabriel, blow—blow the righteous home!

I WANT TO BE AN ANGEL [10]
Plantation Song

I want to be an angel
And with the angels stand,
A crown upon my forehead,
A harp in my hand.Outshine the sun!
Outshine the sun!
Outshine the sun!
And that's the Beulah Land.

MY MOTHER DIED A-SHOUTING [11]
(Plantation Song)

My mother died a-shouting,
I hope she's gone to glory.
The last words I heard her say,
Was about Jerusalem.

About Jerusalem, about Jerusalem,
I'm traveling to the grave Lord,
To lay this body down.

DON'T STAY AWAY, PEOPLE[12]

People, don't stay away,
People, don't stay away;
My Lord says there's room in heaven for all;
My Lord says there's room in heaven for all.

People, don't stay away.
People, don't stay away.
My Lord says there's room in heaven for all;
Room enough in heaven, room enough in heaven for all.

BROTHER I GOT JESUS
(Plantation Song)

If you got Jesus hold him fast.
  Brother I got Jesus!
If you got Jesus hold him fast.
  Brother I got Jesus!
I had a mighty struggle, but I got it at last.
  Brother I got Jesus!
I had a mighty struggle, but I got it at last.
  Brother I got Jesus!

TURN, SINNER, TURN
(Prisoners' Song)

Turn, sinner, turn; turn to God and live;
Let the dungeon chuck and the chains fall off,
Turn to God and live.

I never was so low before,

As when I lay at hell's dark door;
Turn, sinner, turn; turn to God and live.

O, when Jesus spoke unto my soul,
I felt like a feather in the air;
Turn, sinner, turn; turn to God and live.

O, I felt like a feather in the air,
When Jesus spoke unto my soul;
Turn, sinner turn; turn to God and live.

JESUS IS THE LIGHT

Jesus is the Light, the Light of the world,
Jesus is the Light, the Light of the world,
He shines all round us, both night and day,
Jesus is the Light of the world.

Hark ye, say the angels, Jesus is the Light of the world;
Hark ye, say the angels, Jesus is the Light of the world;
Hark ye, say the angels, Jesus is the Light of the world;
He shines all round us, both night and day.

HE BROUGHT ME FROM A LONG, LONG WAY

Oh, he bro't me from de rocking of my cradle,
He bro't me from a long, long way.
Oh, he bro't me from de rocking of my cradle,
He bro't me from a long, long way.

Oh, he shoed my feet for a journey,
An he bro't me from a long, long way.
Oh, he shoed my feet for a journey,
An he bro't me from a long, long way.

Oh, he bro't me from de rocking of my cradle,
He bro't me from a long, long way.

Oh, he bro't me from de rocking of my cradle,
He bro't me from a long, long way.

Oh, he clothed me when I was naked,
He bro't me from a long, long way.
He clothed me when I was naked,
He bro't me from a long, long way.

Oh, he bro't me from de rocking of my cradle,
An'he bro't me from a long, long way.
Oh, he bro't me from de rocking of my cradle,
Oh he bro't me from a long, long way.

YOU CAN FIND ME UP THERE

If you miss me from singing,
And can't find me no where,
Jist come on up to sweet heaben,
I'll be singing up dere.

You can find me up dere,
You can find me up dere,
Jist come on up to sweet heaben,
You can find me up dere.

If you miss me from praying,
And can't find me no where,
Jist come on up to sweet heaben,
I'll be prayin up dere.

If you miss me from shoutin,
And can't find me no where,
Jist come on up to sweet heaben,
I'll be shoutin up dere.

GO ON DEACON AND GET YOUR CROWN[14]

Go on, deacon, and get your crown,
Go on, deacon, and get your crown,
Go on, deacon, and get your crown,
The house of the Lord I'm bound for.

My soul is bound for glory, yes, Lord, glory,
My soul is bound for glory, yes, Lord, glory,
That's what satan is a-grumbling about.

I'M STANDIN' ON A SOLID ROCK

I'm standin' on a solid Rock, and it won't give away.
I'm standin' on a solid Rock, and it won't give away.
I'm standin' on a solid Rock, and it won't give away.
Lord, I need you everywhere I go.

My mother says it's a solid Rock, and it won't give away.
My mother says it's a solid Rock, and it won't give away.
My mother says it's a solid Rock, and it won't give away.
Lord, I need you everywhere I go.

My pastor says it's a solid Rock, and it won't give away.
My pastor says it's a solid Rock, and it won't give away.
My pastor says it's a solid Rock, and it won't give away.
Lord, I need you everywhere I go.

My deacon says it's a solid Rock, and it won't give away.
My deacon says it's a solid Rock, and it won't give away.
My deacon says it's a solid Rock, and it won't give away.
Lord, I need you everywhere I go.

Chorus:

I'm standin' on a solid Rock, and it won't give away.
I'm standin' on a solid Rock, and it won't give away.
I'm standin' on a solid Rock, and it won't give away.
Lord, I need you everywhere I go.

I ' M   A   R U N N I N G   F O R   M Y   L I F E

I'm a runnin' for my life.
I'm a runnin' for my life.
If anybody ask you
What's de matter with me,
Just tellum I say-a
I'm a runnin' for my life.

I'm a moanin' for my life.
I'm a moanin' for my life.
If anybody ask you
What's de matter with me,
Just tellum I say-a
I'm a runnin' for my life.

I'm a prayin' for my life.
I'm a prayin' for my life.
If anybody ask you
What's de matter with me,
Just tellum I say-a
I'm a runnin' for my life.

I'm a runnin' for my life.
I'm a runnin' for my life.
If anybody ask you
What's de matter with me,
Just tellum I say-a
I'm a runnin' for my life.

K E E P   I N C H I N '   A L O N G

Keep inchin' along, like a poor inch worm.
Keep inchin' along, like a poor inch worm.
Jesus a-comin' bye and bye.
Keep inchin' along, keep inchin' along,
Jesus a-comin' bye and bye.

Satan is like a snake in de grass,
Always in some Christian path.
Keep inchin' along, keep inchin' along,
Jesus is comin' bye and bye.

Keep inchin' along, keep inchin' along,
Keep inchin' along, like a poor inch worm.
Jesus is comin' bye and bye.
Keep inchin' along, keep inchin' along,
Jesus is comin' bye and bye.

LITTLE MOSES[15]

Down by that river so clear,
The ladies were wending their way
When Pharaoh's daughter
Stepped down in the water
To bathe in the cool of the day.

They opened the ark and found a
Sweet infant was there
And Moses looked sad and he cried.
They sent for his mother,
His sister and brother,
And Moses looked glad and he smiled.

NOT SO PARTICLAR 'BOUT SHAKIN' DE HAND

I have a mother in de promis' land;
I'm not so particlar 'bout shakin' her hand;
But I heard an angel singin'.

Oh, let her fly, let her fly,
Lord, Lord, let her fly.
Let her fly to Mt. Zion and sit down.

I have a father in that promis' land
I'm not so particlar 'bout shakin' his hand
But I heard an angel singin'.

Oh, let him fly, let him fly,
Lord, Lord, let him fly,
Let him fly to Mt. Zion and sit down.

CAN'T HIDE SINNER[16]

Chorus

Can't hide, sinner, can't hide, can't hide, sinner,
Can't hide, can't hide, sinner, can't hide.
You can't hide sinner, you can't hide.

I run to de rocks, can't hide.
De rocks cried out, can't hide.
No hidin' place, can't hide.
You can't hide sinner, you can't hide.

I run to de river, can't hide
De river cried out, can't hide
No hidin' place, can't hide
You can't hide sinner, you can't hide.

I run to de mountain, can't hide.
De mountain cried out, can't hide.
No hidin' place, can't hide.
You can't hide sinner, you can't hide.

WE'RE ALL HERE

When Paul and Silas were in Jail,
    Do thyself no harm!
When Paul and Silas were in Jail,
    Do thyself no harm!

Chorus

> *We're all here, we're all here,*
> *Do thyself no harm!*
> *We're all here, we're all here,*
> *Do thyself no harm!*

WHEN I'M GONE

When I'm gone, gone, gone
When I'm gone to come no more,
Church, I know you goin' to miss me
When I'm gone.

You goin' to miss me for my walk,
You goin' to miss me for my walk.
Church, I know you goin' to miss me
When I'm gone.

You goin' to miss me for my talk.
You goin' to miss me for my talk.
Church, I know you goin' to miss me
When I'm gone.

When I'm gone, gone, gone,
When I'm gone to come no more,
Church, I know you goin' to miss me
When I'm gone.

I'M GOING TO TELL IT

I'm goin' to tell it everywhere I go,
I'm goin' to tell it everywhere I go,
I'm goin' to tell it everywhere I go,
How Jesus bless' my soul.

One mornin' I was a-walkin a-long
Jesus, bless my soul.
I heard a voice and saw no one
Jesus, bless my soul.

I'm goin' to tell it everywhere I go,
I'm goin' to tell it everywhere I go,
I'm goin' to tell it everywhere I go,
How Jesus bless' my soul.

I went in de valley, didn't go to stay,
Jesus, bless my soul.
My soul got happy I stayed all day,
Jesus bless' my soul.

MOTHERLESS CHILD

As I walk from door to door,
And I have no where to go,
And I hear my neighbors cry,
That's a motherless child.

As I go from door to door,
Motherless child, motherless child,
Everybody turn me down,
Motherless child.

As I walk thru' the streets,
Yes, my knee bones they seem weak,
For I am hungry and I'm cryin'
Motherless child.

As I walk from door to door,
And I have no where to go,
And I hear my neighbors cry
That's a motherless child.

CHRISTIAN, FIGHT ON, YO' TIME AIN'T LONG

Christian, fight on, yo' time ain't long.
Christian, fight on, yo' time ain't long,
I step in de water and de water was cold,
It chilled my body, but not my soul.
Christian, fight on, yo' time ain't long.

I've been 'buked, and I've been scorned,
I've been talked about as shure as you born,
Christian, fight on, yo' time ain't long.
Christian, fight on, yo' time ain't long.

I COULDN'T REST CONTENTED, UNTIL I FOUND THE LORD

I moaned and I moaned, I moaned and I moaned,
Until I found the Lord.
My soul, I couldn't rest contented, my soul.
I couldn't rest contented until I found the Lord.

I prayed and I prayed, Lord, I prayed and I prayed,
Lord, I prayed and I prayed, until I found the Lord,
My soul, I couldn't rest contented, my soul,
I couldn't rest contented until I found the Lord.

I cried and I cried, I cried and I cried,
I cried and I cried, Lord, I cried and I cried,
Until I found the Lord.
My soul, I couldn't rest contented, my soul,
I couldn't rest contented until I found the Lord.

IV. ENGLISH AND SCOTTISH SONGS[17]

BARB'RY ALLEN

Lonely was a town, a town
Where three fair maids were dwelling,
There was but one I called my own,
And that was Barb'ry Allen.

He sent his servants to the town
Where those three maids were dwelling,
"My Master's sick; he's very sick,
"And it's for you he's dyin'."

Slowly, slowly she got up
And to his bedside going
She drew the curtain to the side
And said, "Young man, you're dyin'."

As she went wailing through the field
She heard her death bell tolling.
She looked to east, and then to west
And saw his corpse a-comin'."

"Lay down, lay down the corpse," she wailed,
"So I may kiss upon him."
The more she kissed the more she grieved,
And busted out a-cryin'.

"O mother, mother, make my bed,
"O make it long and narrow.
"Sweet William died for me today;
"I'll die for him tomorrow."

Sweet William died on Saturday night
And Barb'ry died on Sunday.
The old woman died for the love of both
And was buried Easter Monday.

AUNT TABBY
(Lullabye)

Go tell Aunt Tabby,
Go tell Aunt Ta-a-by,
Go tell Aunt Tabby,
Her old gray goose is dead.

The one she's been saving,
The one she's been s-a-ving,
The one she's been saving,
To make a feather bed.

THE THREE RAVENS

There were three crows sat on a tree.
And they were black as crows can be.
Said one old crow unto his chum,
"What shall we do for chewing gum?

"There lies a horse on yonder plain
"By some cruel butcher was he slain.
"We'll perch upon his raw backbone,
"And pick his eyes out one by one."

GEORGE GILES
(A variant of the Giles Collins ballad.)

George Giles rode home one cold winter night,
George Giles rode home so fine;
George Giles rode home one cold winter night,
And was taken sick and died.

"Oh, I wish to the Lord I'd never been born,
"Or died when I was young,
"Then I'd never been here to weep and to mourn
"The death of my poor George."

"O Daughter, daughter, why do you weep?
"There's plenty more boys like George."
"O father, father, George has my heart,
"And now we forever must part."

"Oh see that yonder turtledove
"Flying from pine to pine
"A-mourning for his lost true love
"And I must mourn for mine."

"No friends, dear friends, I bid you farewell;
"I'm goin' to the shade of the pine
"And there I'm goin' to take my life,
"And rest by my poor George."

COME ALL YOU FAIR
AND PRETTY LADIES

Come all you fair and pretty ladies;
Take warning how you love young men.
They'll shine like a flower on some summer's morning;
They'll shine so bright, but they'll soon decay.

They'll tell to you some love-like story;
They'll tell you that they love you well;
But the way they'll go and court another,
And say their love is not for you.

I wish I were some little swallow,
And one of those had wings to fly,
Wherever you might go that I might follow,
And in his breast that I might flutter.

I am not no little swallow,
Nor none of these have wings to fly.
I'll stay down here and sleep and slumber,
And sing and pass my time away.

A RAILROAD BOY

In New York town there once did dwell
A railroad boy; I love him well.
He courted me my life away,
And now with me he will not stay.

There is another place in town
Where he often goes and sits around;
He'll take some strange girl upon his knee.
He'll tell her things he won't tell me.

It's grief, oh, grief, I'll tell you why;
It's because she has more gold than I.
Her gold will melt, her beauty fly,
And she'll be as poor as I.

So dig my grave both wide and deep,
Place a marble stone at my head and feet;
Upon my breast a lonesome dove
To show this world that I died for love.

THE JEWELER'S DAUGHTER

It rains, it pours, it rains, it pours,
It rains both night and day.
The prettiest boy in our whole town
Came down there playing ball.

They tossed the ball so high, so low,
And then again so low;
They tossed it onto the jeweler's daughter,
Dressed in green and yellow,
"Come in, come in, my pretty little boy,
"And get your ball again."

"I can't and I shan't and I can't come in,
"Without my playmates all,

"For that would get to my mother's ears;
"Her tears would surely fall."

She showed to him an apple seed,
And then a bright gold ring;
She showed him a cherry rose-red,
And that's what 'ticed him in.

She took him by his lily-white hand,
And led him through the wall;
She led him into the chamber room,
Where none could hear him call.

She pinned him in a silver chair;
She pinned him with a pin
She brought a basin bright and brass
For to catch his heart's blood in.

O nurse me, nurse me, now or never,
O nurse me now or never;
If I ever live to be a man,
I'll give you a veil forever.

V. TWO GEORGIA CRIMES

FRANK DUPREE

Now I want my buddies and all my friends
To take this warning from me;
Stop your drinking, buddies, and live like men;
Don't live like Frank Dupree.

I went to Atlanta with my sweetheart fair;
I stopped at a jewelry store.
I took this diamond while standing there,
But I'll not take no more.

I took this diamond and I left that shop;
I stepped out on the street;
I pulled my pistol and I shot that cop;
I laid him dead at my feet.

They had me arrested, and I went to trial;
At last the judge did say,
"Lo! Frank Dupree is nothing but a child,
"But he's thrown his life away."

"Come here, buddies, and come here quick,
"And see the last of this one;
"See what the smoking of fine cigarettes
"And a sporting life has done."

LITTLE MARY FAGAN[18]

Poor Mary Fagan left her home one gloomy April day.
She went to the pencil factory to draw her little pay.
A wicked man was waiting there for he knew very well
That if she left the place alive a story she would tell.

Poor Mary's mother wept and mourned, for her poor child was gone.
She tried to save her honor and her life she gave.
And now she's gone to heaven; forever she's at rest.
Safe in the arms of Jesus now, safe on his gentle breast.

SOURCES

1. Sung by Negro section hand. Field Worker: George Paulk. Nov., 1936.
2. Sung by Negro section hand. Field Worker: George Paulk. Nov., 1936.
3. Sung by ex-slave. Field Worker: Louise Oliphant. Augusta.
4. Field Worker: N. B. Swilling, Note accompanying song reads "I heard a Negro wash woman sing this song when I was a child."
5. Sung by Homer Kemp, ex-slave. Marietta.
6. Sung by Robert Kimbrough, ex-slave. Columbus. Dec., 1936.
7. Sung by Robert Kimbrough, ex-slave. Columbus, Dec., 1936.
8. Sung by ex-slave. Field Worker: Louise Oliphant. Augusta.

9. Sung by Robert Kimbrough, ex-slave. Columbus, Dec., 1936.
10. Sung by ex-slave. Field Worker: Louise Oliphant. Augusta.
11. Sung by ex-slave. Field Worker: Louise Oliphant. Augusta.
12. Sung by Robert Kimbrough, ex-slave. Columbus. Dec., 1936.
13. Sung by ex-slave. Field Worker: Louise Oliphant. Augusta.
14. Sung by ex-slave. Field Worker: Louise Oliphant. Augusta.
15. Sung by Georgia mountaineer. Rabun and Habersham Counties.
16. Sung by Mary Ferguson, ex-slave. Columbus. Dec., 1936.
17. The WPA field workers culled suprisingly few English and Scottish ballads in their work. The editors conjecture that the few which are included in the manuscripts found their way there because the collectors thought them indigenous.
18. This song, dealing with the murder of a Marietta girl, was added to the folklore files in 1950 by Marvin McCloud. Mary Phagan was murdered in a pencil factory in ~~1933.~~ 1913.

INDEX